O'NEILL

PEOPLE AND PLACES

by

Sean O'Neill

BALLINAKELLA PRESS

1991

ISBN 0 946538 04 2

Series Editor: Hugh W. L. Weir
Typesetting and layout: Grania R. Weir, Tomas J. Porcell
Design, Maps and Line drawings: Aodh de Mheir

Acknowledgements

Thanks are due to the Irish Architectural Archives (Illustration of Shane's Castle), the Tate Gallery, London (Wright's portrait of Sir Niall O'Neill), the Mercier Press (Chief O'Neill's Favourite Song) for permission to use their material.   The Western Library Board of N. Ireland (Harry Avery's Castle) and Anne Loane, Kathleen Neill, Don Carlos O'Neill and Don Hugo O'Neill, Ua Neill Mor and Ua Neill Buidhe respectively, Grania R. Weir, Tomas J. Porcell and Hugh W. L. Weir etc. as well as to the printers and bookbinders, Messrs. Colour Books Ltd.

CONTENTS

* ILLUSTRATED

A Widespread and Significant Race

In Ireland a surname either connects one to more than a thousand years of history or to three hundred years of attempted domination. Each Gaelic-Irish surname has its pantheon of heroes and its list of "villains". The O'Neill surname has a long history. Its bearers are and have been varied and widespread. The villains could be construed to be those O'Neills who served the interests of the Normans in the south of Ireland, those few who turned protestant and embraced Anglo-Saxon culture, the O'Neills who gave up their ancient titles in exchange for English Earldoms or even that clansman who is supposed to have shot Michael Collins in 1922. The heroes of the surname might be those who gave their lives for cause of Irish Gaeldom and Nationalism, the Nobel Prize winner for Literature, the O'Neill who founded a small city, a horse racing jockey who became a champion in Britain, the O'Neills who became Governors of the States of Alabama and Connecticut or even "Tip" O'Neill, who became Speaker of the House of Representatives in the United States Congress (the third most important political position in the U.S.A.).

The surname O'Neill has been used in somewhat unconventional ways. Some members of the American mafia used it as an alias and the modern I.R.A. are known to use it in their pronouncements to the media.

Apart from the chieftains of the Clan who bear the titles Ua Neill Mor and Ua Neill Buidhe, bearers of the name have been Kings, Princes, Marquesses, Earls, Counts, Barons and Baronets. O'Neills have always been active in military service and have held the highest ranks of Field Marshall and General. Until his retirement in 1989, the former Chief of Staff of the Irish Army was Lt. General Tadgh O'Neill of Wexford.

No matter what their station in life, almost all O'Neills could eventually trace their ancestry back to the various O'Neill groups and major families that have spread throughout Ireland and the World. The Lord Mayoralty of Dublin was once held by a Laurence O'Neill but today there are very few, if any, O'Neills active in Irish politics. Most O'Neills are involved in Business, the Arts, Law, Medicine, Military Service and Sport.

This short volume is a potpourri of O'Neill places and characters. Their collective history would cover countless volumes but it is hoped that this account will encourage further exploration of O'Neill ancestry and will point genealogical researchers and general readers in the right direction.

The O'Neills in the Annals

It would be impossible to cover the extensive references to O'Neills in the Irish Annals but there are several O'Neills whose contribution should be mentioned. Reference is made to Domnall Ua Neill between the years A.D. 943-979. He was King of Ireland and the first to use the surname O'Neill. In A.D. 953 he campaigned in the vicinity of the Rivers Blackwater and Bann and made war on the O Rourkes of Breffny. Seven years later he went on a circuit of Ireland with his army. He stayed three days at Rath Edain, which was probably an area in the present Barony of Idrone, Co. Carlow. It is difficult to understand how O'Neills, supposedly of Ulster (as recorded in some sources), managed to have a territory in Carlow from such an early date as the 10th century. An "Ua Neill a Magh da chonn" is recorded in the Caithreim Ceallachan Caisil and in the Annals of the Four Masters. These O'Neills are almost certainly members of the Ui Chennselaig Tribe of Leinster.

In A.D. 961 Domnall Ua Neill, King of Ireland, attacked the crannogs in the Lakes of Westmeath and five years later plundered most of Leinster. In A.D. 968 he attacked the Monastery of Mainister Buithe in Co. Louth before plundering Co. Offaly the following year. His rule ended in A.D. 979. His son, Maelseachlainn Ua Neill, reigned as Monarch for about twenty years from A.D. 980 . In A.D. 989 he defeated the foreigners (Norsemen) of Ath Cliath (Dublin) and thereafter each resident of the settlement was required to pay an ounce of gold to the O'Neill dynasty. This was wildly optimistic of Maelseachlainn and it is doubtful if this tribute was paid for more than a few years. In A.D. 998 he expelled Sitric, the Viking-Irish King, from his Kingdom of Ath Cliath. This O'Neill lost the crown of Ireland to the O'Briens when Brian Boru (Boroimhe - of the tributes) brought the nation together in A.D. 1001. Brian had invited the O'Neills of Ulster to assist him at the Battle of Clontarf but they declined. One O'Neill, Felim "of the Silver Shield" did, however, fight with Brian at this confrontation which took place in 1014.

In A.D. 1100 the O'Neills lost more power when the Clann Donaill (the MacLochlainns) took the Kingship of Cineal Eoghain from them but, after a period of one hundred and forty one years, the O'Neills regained it. Brian Rua O Neill finally defeated the MacLochlainns in 1241 and his clan reigned again until circa 1603. This territory was known variously as Telach Oc, Tulach Og, Tullaghoge, Aileach, Cineal Eoghain, Tir Eoghain, Tyrone and Ulster over several hundred years.

Some Significant O'Neill Events

978   Death of Domnall Ua Neill, King of Ireland, (grandson of [Ua] Niall Glundubh), first to use surname, Ua Neill or O'Neill.

1001 Maelseachlainn, last "Ua Neill" King of Ireland, deposed.

1014 Felim O Neill, "of the Silver Shield", fought at Clontarf.

1036 Death of Flaithbertach, King of Aileach. Made a pilgrimage to Rome in 1030.

1196 Aodh O Neill, King of Cineal Eoghain, fought the Normans.

1283 Aodh Buidhe O Neill, founder of the O'Neills of Clanaboy, killed.

1476 Henry, the "O'NEILL" demolished Belfast Castle.

1542 Con Bacach, the "O'NEILL", was created First Earl of Tyrone.

1574 Sir Bryan Mac Phelim O'Neill, "Ua Neill Buidhe", was killed by the Earl of Essex.

1616 Death of Hugh, the "O'NEILL", second Earl of Tyrone, third Baron of Dungannon.

1641 Donagh and Hugh O Neill (Ui Neill a Magh da chonn) owned 1,200 acres in Co. Carlow which was lost during the Cromwellian period.

1649 Eoghan Rua O Neill victor of Benburb, died.

1653 Sir Phelim O Neill, M.P. for Dungannon, hanged.

1660 Death of Hugh, nephew of Hugh O Neill who signed the Treaty of Limerick.

1664 Col. Sir Daniel O Neill, British Postmaster General, died.

1690 Henry O'Neill/Paine, founded the Cork "O'NEILLS".

1700 Art og O Neill/Paine, was made "O'NEILL" (of the Fews).

1765 Birth of Padraig O Neill, genealogist and antiquarian, of the Ui Neill a Uibh Eoghain Fhinn.

1777 Birth of John O'Neill, poet. His most famous work was 'The Drunkard'.

1798 John O'Neill, Viscount and Baron, killed by a pikeman.

1805 Arturo O'Neill, made Marques del Norte by the King of Spain.

1834 John O'Neill, Inspector General of the I.R.A. (America) born.

1936 Eugene O'Neill awarded Nobel Prize for Literature. He died 1953.

1953 Death of Rose Cecil O'Neill, millionaire, inventor of the "KEWPIE DOLL".

1989 Retirement of Lt. General Tadgh O'Neill from County Wexford, Irish Army Chief of Staff.

1990 Death of Terence O'Neill, Baron O'Neill of the Maine, former Northern Ireland Prime Minister, of the Chichester-O'Neill family.

O'Neill Titles of Nobility or Election
(Ulster, Magh da chonn and Uibh Eoghain)

King of Ireland
King of Ulster
King of Telach Oc
King of Aileach

Principe de Ultonia
Prince of Tir Eoghain
Prince of Trian Congall

Lord Mac Martin
Lord Mac John
Lord of the Fews
Lord of Magh da chonn
Lord of Uibh Eoghain Fhinn
Lord of the Feeva
Lord of Kilultagh

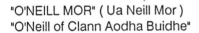

"O'NEILL MOR" (Ua Neill Mor)
"O'Neill of Clann Aodha Buidhe"

Governor of Kinnard / Kinard

Marques de Valdeosera
Marques de Caltojar
Marques de la Granja
Marques de Vincent
Marques del Norte

Earl of Tyrone
Earl O'Neill
Earl of Clanconnell
Conde de Banajiar
Conde de Tiron
Comte de Tyrone
Count de Raymond
Count Thomas O'Neill

Viscount O'Neill
Visconde de Santa Monica

Baron of Dungannon
Baron O'Neill
Baron O'Neill of the Maine
Baron O'Neill of Shane's Castle
Baron Rathcavan
Baron Clogher

Baronet of Upper Claneboys

Knight of Calatrava
Knight of Malta
Knight of the Rose of Brazil
Knight of the Order of Christ
Knight de la Maestranza
Knight of Santiago
Knight of the Military Order of
  Carlos III

The Arms, Crests, Mottos and war cries of the O'Neills

Amongst the Gaelic-Irish, heraldry was little used until the 15th and 16th centuries. Genealogy was more important because many male members of the family were entitled to succeed to the chieftainship. In heraldic terms the simplest form of O'Neill arms is, "Argent a sinister red hand couped at the wrist affrontes gules". "The red hand is always the most important element. These were said to have been inherited from the old Irian Kings of Ulster. Many brances of the O'Neills have their own arms but most have embellishments such as crowns, mullets, salmon, strawberry leaves, lions and "waves of the sea". The salmon supposedly represents O'Neill sovereignity over Lough Neagh but is more likely to come from a symbol used by the O Cathains. They had the right to throw the 'golden' shoe over the O'Neill's head at the inauguration at Tullaghoge , (there is some doubt whether it was O'Cathain or O Hagan). Certainly, they were close to the O'Neills and were one of the O'Neill's Ur-Ri (subsidiary Kings or Lords). The salmon occurs on a tombstone belonging to a thirteenth century O Cathain, Prince of Limavady, in Dungiven Church. Early O'Neill symbols were red hands on signet rings, a mounted King with drawn sword and a shield with a right hand extended, supported by two lions. The most eleborate coats of arms belong to the hereditary O'Neill of Clann Aodha Buidhe, "In chief argent a dexter hand couped and erect, supported by two lions rampant surmounted by three mullets, the whole gules, the base waves of the sea propper. Whereon a salmon naiant propper, the shield is surmounted by the mediaeval princely crown of three strawberry leaves.
Crest: A dexter hand in armour embowed propper garnished or, holding in the hand a dagger also propper pommel and hilt gold.
Motto: Coelo, Solo, Salo, Potentes.
War Cry: Lamh dearg Eireann abu (the red hand of Ireland forever),and to the Prince of Tyrone, "argent two lions rampant gules armed and langued az. supporting a sinister red hand couped at the wrist erect, palm outward."
Crest: A right arm couped below the elbow cased grasping a naked sword.
Motto: Lamh Dearg Abu (The red hand forever).
Similar O'Neill arms to these include those of the Barons Dungannon, the Earls of Tyrone and the O'Neills of Shane's Castle. The O'Neills of Leitrim and Mayo (originally of the Fews) had a slightly different crest and motto. Their crest is: "a naked arm embowed brandishing a sword all propper", and their motto, "Haec manus pro patriae rugnando vulnera passa". (This hand has been wounded in defence of my country). The "O'Neill Mor" , Don Carlos, has an even more elaborate escutcheon.

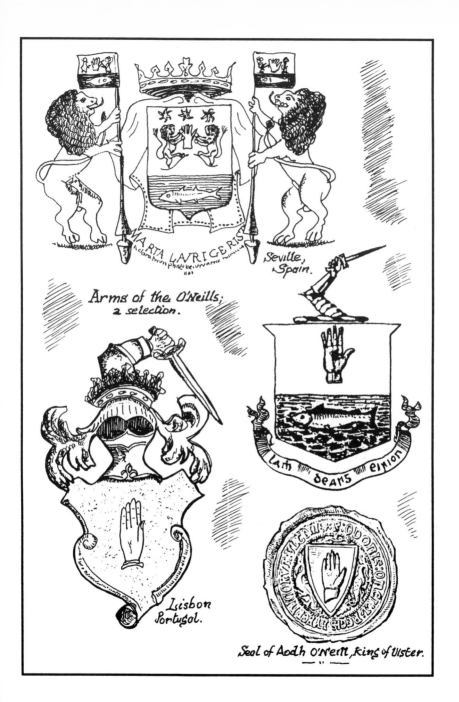

ARTA LAVRICERIS

Seville, Spain.

Arms of the O'Neills;
a selection.

lam deans einion

Lisbon
Portugal.

Seal of Aodh O'Neill, King of Ulster.

The Grianan of Aileach, Co. Donegal

During the fifth century the Ui Neill moved into the area now known as Donegal. From them stem the three septs: the Cineal Eoghain, the Cineal Conaill and the Cineal Enna. The Cineal Enna disappeared into obscurity but the other two developed the Ir territories of Inis Eoghain (Inishowen) and Tir Conaill (Tyrconnell). From these septs descend the O'Neills, the O'Donnells and the O'Dohertys. The Ui Neill were referred to as Kings of Aileach when mentioned in the early Annals. Their ancient habitation and inauguration site was the Grianan of Aileach. Grianan means "a palace, a royal seat or a sunny place". The Grianan of Aileach is situated on top of the Greenan mountain on the Inishowen peninsula a few miles west of Derry. It is a cashel or earthen ring fort enclosed by massive walls of drystone construction. The whole consists of three enclosing earthen banks and has been restored. A rectangular structure once stood in the centre but this is no longer visible. In the immediate area there is also a tumulus, an ancient road and a holy well dedicated to St. Patrick.

The Grianan was rebuilt and restored by Dr. Walter Bernard of Derry between 1874 and 1878. It is thought that the rectangular central structure which once stood within its walls was an 18th century penal chapel.

This O'Neill inauguration site was attacked by norsemen in A.D. 939 and Muircheartach Ua Neill, Prince of Aileach, was taken prisoner. He escaped soon after. At the beginning of the 12th century the Grianan of Aileach was dismantled by Murtagh O Brien, King of Munster, in revenge for the destruction of that family's "Palace of Kincora" in County Clare. Soon after this episode, the MacLochlainns (1100-1241), and the O'Neills made Telach Oc (Tullaghoge) in County Tyrone their inauguration site. The O'Neills used the latter site until the end of the 16th century.

Some O'Neills, calling the members of their family by the surname Paine, did use the Grianan for inaugurations of themselves as "O'NEILLS" and Princes of Tyrone in the 18th century but it was never "officially" used again by O'Neills since its plunder in the 10th century.

An Grianan - Exterior and interior views.

Tullaghoge

Tullaghoge, the ancient O'Neill inauguration site, is situated between Cookstown and Stewartstown in County Tyrone. There has been no O'Neill inauguration there since that of Hugh, "The Great", O'Neill late in the 16th century. The site consists of the O'Hagan rath (which is at present overgrown with trees), the O'Hagan burial ground and the O'Neill inauguration site. This site is situated half way down the hill from the rath. It consists of a very peculiar and impressive stone which is a part of the hill itself. This is where the three sandstone slabs were placed around the stone to represent a chair. Lord Mountjoy had these slabs destroyed in 1602 due to his impression that they were an important part of the site. In all references to this site there is no mention of a "chair" but of a "stone" and since this was also called the "Leac na Ri", we can be certain that the surviving "stone" at Tullaghoge is that stone.

The "O'Neill" was inaugurated with traditional ceremony. The chieftain and his vassels would gather in a local church and then parade along a pathway leading up to and through the O'Hagan rath. The "O'Neill" would sit on the stone which had been made to resemble a chair. O'Cahan and O'Hagan played the most important roles in the ceremony. One threw the golden or brass shoe over The O'Neill's head and another placed the rod, a symbol of authority, in his hand. It is thought that the O'Neill then stood up and turned "thrice forward and backward"; observing his territory as he did so. However, this is impossible to do standing on the present stone, mainly because of its situation on the slope of a hill. It is still exactly where one would expect it to be according to the Bartlett map of 1602, though.

In the local Church of Ireland church, there is a small section of one of the sandstone slabs that surrounded the "O'Neill" stone. It is a part of the arch over the doorway into the church which is dated "A.D. 1735". There is also an interesting miniature O'Neill "chair" in the church itself. A fully sized reconstruction of the "chair" is now in the Benburb Heritage centre.

There was also another O'Neill chair at CASTLEREAGH, an area of farmland near Belfast. This chair was taken from its site to Belfast before being transfered to Sligo. There it was cared for by Mr. J. Walker. A Mr. S. Millagan arranged, in or around 1898, to have it taken to the Ulster Museum in Belfast where it is now preserved and protected. It had been hoped that this chair would have been used in the "O'Neill of Clann Aodha Buidhe" ceremony in 1982 but permission was withheld by the Trustees of the Museum.

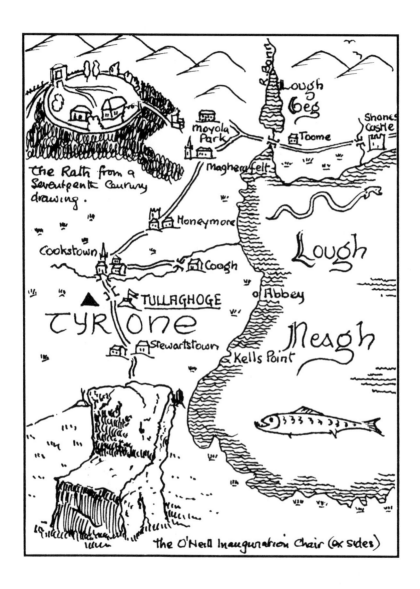

the Rath from a Seventeenth Century drawing.

Cookstown

Moyola Park

Maghera felt

Lough Beg

Toome

Shanes Castle

Honeymore

Coagh

TULLAGHOGE

TYRONE

o Abbey

Lough

Stewartstown

Kells Point

Neagh

the O'Neill Inauguration Chair (ox sides)

Aodh Buidhe O Neill

Aodh, King of Aileach and King of Cineal Eoghain (1260-83), was the son of Domnall O Neill who was slain in 1234. During his principality he moved into the area consisting of the present counties Antrim and Down which thereafter became known as the territory of the O'Neills of Clann Aodha Buidhe. This was later anglicised to Clanaboy (Clandeboy). In 1533, the area was divided into two O'Neill territories. Muircheartach received Lower Clanaboy and Aodh took over Upper Clanaboy. The northern part consisted of what are the present baronies of the two Antrims, the two Toomes, the two Belfasts, lower Massareene and the town of Carrickfergus. The southern part consisted of Upper and Lower Castlereach.

Aodh O Neill, in 1275, was refered to as "Aodh O Neill regem de Kinelowen" or King of Cineal Eoghain. A silver seal with the inscription "Sigillum Odonis O Neill regis Hiberniae coran Ultoniae" is said to be connected with this Aodh. The "Odonis" is perported to be an attempt to Latinise the name Aodh (see page 4). Eight years later, Aodh O Neill was murdered by Brian Mac Mahon, King of Oriel and of Gillaiosa (Monaghan). He was succeeded by his son Brian O Neill, Prince of Tyrone and Clanaboy, (Tir Eoghain agus Clann Aodha Buidhe), who was slain in 1295.

The O'Neills of Clann Aodha Buidhe maintained sovereign control over their territory from the time of Aodha Buidhe until the middle of the 17th century. The O'Neill family of this clan survived at Shane's Castle and at Edenduffcarrick until the middle of the 19th century. This was mainly because they had become Protestant and had become anglicised. One of them became Grandmaster of the Orange Order. The last two of these O'Neills in the male line died unmarried and childless in 1841 and 1855 respectively.

The Clan of Aodha Buidhe O Neill has not died out. It is nowadays represented by a Roman Catholic Portugese businessman, Hugo O'Neill, chief of his name and "O Neill of Clann Aodha Buidhe".

Harry Avery's Castle

As one approaches Newtownstewart on the road from Derry to Omagh, one can see the impressive ruins of Harry Avery's Castle situated on a hill above the town. The present day remains of this fortress, named after Einri Aimbreidh O'Neill who died in 1392, consist of the main rectangular entrance block, at the ends of which and facing to the front are two huge semi circular towers.   The original bailly and its surrounding two metre high curtain wall still lineate the castle bawn.   Traces of wattle plasterwork can still be observed in the low vaulted chambers of each tower. The castle was destroyed in 1609 and the stones used in its building have been taken for use in other local structures ever since. To the north and west are the traces of the contemporary deerpark which would have been used for hunting and food provision. Einri was the second son of Neil Mor who was styled "Le Grand O'Neill" by the Normans while by the Irish ,he was named "The Defender of Ireland", "the Unyeilding Tower Against Tyranny".   Einri's father survived him and was to meet King Richard II of England when he visited Dundalk in 1394. Neil Mor's wife was Gormley, daughter of John O'Donnell. She died in 1397.

Shane's Castle, Co. Antrim

Shane's Castle was named after Shane Mac Bryan O'Neill who was the last Prince of Clann Aodha Buidhe in the time of King James I (1603 - 25).   Until then, the 12th century building had been called Edan Dubh Carrig or Edenduffcarrick ("the black face of the rock").   In the 19th century, the owner related that this name referred to a face chiselled into a rock which was incorporated into a southern turret of the now ruined castle which stands on an elevated plateau on the north eastern shore of Lough Neagh.   Shane's son, Sir Henry O'Neill, got a patent for the four Lordships of Edenduffcarrick, Mullaghan, Largy and Braid from James I.   In 1637 these estates were entailed on Bryan Mac Hugh og O'Neill, Lord of the Feeva to the north.   He was the grandson of Henry's uncle and of Shane's brother, Con Mac Bryan O'Neill.

Seventy-nine years later, the Lordships were inherited by Sean an Francaigh; otherwise known as "French" John O'Neill because of the amount of time he spent in France.   John was the grandson of Phelim Duff.   "French" John's grandson, John O'Neill, born in 1740, sat for the family borough of Randalstown in the Irish House of Commons and supported catholic emancipation.   He was created a Baron in 1793, a Viscount in 1795 and was Governor of Antrim three years later.   He was killed by a pikeman in Antrim in 1798.   By his wife, Henrietta Boyle, daughter of Lord Dungarvan, he had two sons: St. John and John Bruce Richard O'Neill.   Charles Henry became an Earl in 1800, joint Postmaster General of Ireland in 1807 and Lord Lieutenant of Antrim in 1831.   He was also Grandmaster for Ireland of the Orange Order.   In or about 1815 he attempted to remove a graveyard from an area close to his house at Shane's Castle but the local people resented his action.   Whether it was due to this or as a result of a bird's nest catching fire in the chimney, the castle was burnt down in 1816.   The fire, strangely, was started in the room called the "Banshee's Room".   The Banshee of the O'Neills of Clann Aodha Buidhe was known as "Kathleen" and she was said to have slept on a bed in this room.   It is reputed that sometimes an indentation had been noticed on the bed in the morning.   This room was never used but, on the night that it went on fire an exception was made due to an overflow of guests.   The present house is a 19th century building.

Raymond, Lord O'Neill, lives at Shane's Caslte which is nowadays a local tourist attraction.   He participated in and allowed the inauguration of Jorge O'Neill as "O'Neill of Clann Aodha Buidhe" here in 1982. The O'Neills of Shane's Castle are on friendly terms with the Portuguese O'Neills.

Shane's Castle, Antrim, 1894 (Irish Architectural Archives)

Shane the Proud

Shane the Proud (Sean an Diomuis) was born in 1530. His father was Con Bacach (1484-1559), the First Earl of Tyrone, who had submitted to Henry VIII in 1542, having renounced his title of "O'Neill". His mother was probably Mary O'Neill, daughter of Hugh O'Neill of Clann Aodha Buidhe. Shane was "Tanist" or chosen successor to his father and had no interest in using English titles. The English were aware of his sentiments and were preparing Matthew, illegitimate son of Con Bacach and of Alison Kelly, to succeed Con as Earl. To this purpose they created him Baron of Dungannon. Shane refered to him as "Matthew Kelly" and had no intention of allowing him to succeed to his ancestral land and titles. Shane was himself elected "O'Neill" and King of Ulster in 1550. Con Bacach, betrayed by Matthew, was imprisoned. Matthew, on the orders of Shane, was killed in 1558. Con Bacach died in 1559 and as a result, Shane, as "O'Neill" and not as Earl of Tyrone, was actively claiming and taking control of O'Neill territories. Calvach O'Donnell fought against O'Neill's claim but was eventually defeated and taken prisoner in 1559. Shane's vassels were the Magennises, MacArtans, Dufferins, Maguires, MacMahons, O Cahans, O Hanlons, O Hagans, Savages and other O'Neill families.

To show his loyalty and to attempt to stop the English plots to control Ulster, in 1562 he visited Queen Elizabeth I. With him he took his poet, his marshall, his constable and his standard bearer. He reputedly made a great impact on the citizens of London and on Elizabeth's Court but it was to no avail. Elizabeth was secretly trying to rid herself of him.

In 1565 he declared himself "Monarch of Ireland" which explains why the English nicnamed him "Shane the Proud". There followed a protracted war between him and the English forces.

Two years later Shane arranged to meet Alexander Oge MacDonnell of Antrim to try and secure an alliance, but the MacDonnells were sworn enemies of the O'Neills. Alexander had landed at Cushendun after having sailed from Scotland. On arriving, and unknown to Shane, he had met with William Piers, Governor of Carrickfergus. Together they decided the method with which they were to dispose of Shane. A banquet was arranged and pretending an argument, the Scots slew Shane and fifty of his guards.

Shane's body was interred in the Friary of Glenarm in Co. Antrim. His body was exhumed. After a short time, the head was chopped off and brought to Dublin where it was placed on a pole on the walls of Dublin Castle. The rest of the body was reburied in Glenarm.

Shane The Proud.

Turlough Luineach O'Neill

Turlough O'Neill, who was born around 1530, was fostered by O Luinigh of Muintir Luinigh in County Tyrone. For this reason Turlough was given the middle name of Luineach. He was the son of Niall and great grandson of Art Og who was a brother of Con Mor O'Neill. The latter was the father of the more famous Con Bacach O'Neill, the First Earl of Tyrone. Turlough became Tanist to "Shane the Proud". While Shane was responsible for the death of Matthew O'Neill, Baron of Dungannon, the Baron's son Brian, the second Baron of Dungannon, was slain by Turlough in 1562. After the death of "Shane the Proud", Turlough Luineach O Neill became the "O'NEILL". He was inaugurated in 1567.

In 1569, Turlough O'Neill married Agnes Campbell by whom he had a son, Sir Art O'Neill. He had also had a son named Henry by his first wife but he was to have been killed in 1578. In 1572, Sir Thomas Smith attempted the colonisation of O'Neill's territory but he was repulsed by Turlough. Three years later, Turlough had to submit to the Earl of Essex but was regranted lands stretching from Lough Foyle to the Blackwater and from the Bann to Lough Erne.

The titles of Baron Clogher and Earl of Clanconnell were reputedly bestowed on Turlough O'Neill in 1578, but there is some doubt whether they were ever confirmed. Five years after this, Turlough was defeated by the O'Donnells at the Battle of Drumleen.

Throughout his reign, Turlough was under constant pressure from the English favourite, Hugh O'Neill. Hugh was eventually to succeed him as "O'NEILL," but he was defeated by Turlough in 1588. Due to ill health, Turlough resigned as "O'NEILL" in 1593 and received a life interest in the district of Strabane. He died in 1595.

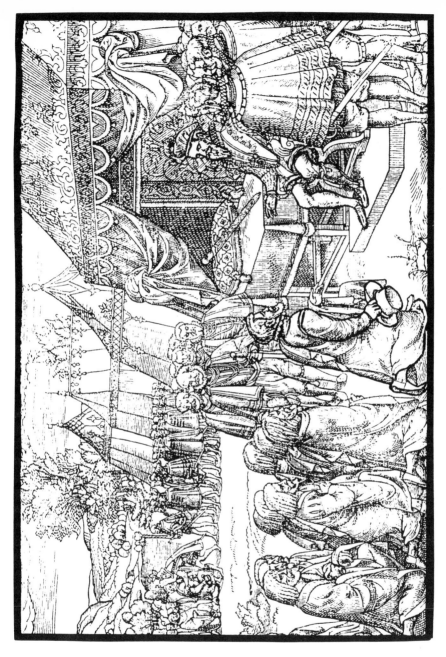

The Submission of Turlough Luineach O'Neill.

"The Great Hugh O'Neill"
(Aodh O Neill)

Hugh, " The Great " O'Neill was born in 1546.   He was the son of Matthew, Baron of Dungannon, the illegitimate son of Con Bachach.   In a secret English conspiracy, Hugh had been brought up from an early age (1562 - 1568) in the Castle of Kenilworth in England, home of Lord Robert Dudley, future Earl of Leicester and favourite of Queen Elizabeth I.   The aim was to turn Hugh into a " little Englishman " and therefore serve the interests of the Crown in Ulster.   Turlough Luineach had succeeded Shane " The Proud " as the "O Neill ".   When Hugh O'Neill returned to Ulster he was allocated land in Armagh.   Turlough raided this territory on many occasions and is said once to have stolen 30,000 cattle belonging to Hugh. Hugh was loyal to the English for a time but a massacre on Rathlin Island, and Elizabeth's constant interest in securing Ulster lands for herself, seems to have changed his loyalties.   Hugh O'Neill began his campaign against the English in 1593.   He won the Battle of the Biscuits in 1594.   After the retirement of Turlough Luineach, he assumed the title of " O'Neill " and discarded the English titles of Earl of Tyrone and Baron of Dungannon in 1593.

Further victories took place at Druimfliuch, 1595, Clontribet, 1595, Benburb, 1597 and at Tyrell's Pass in 1597.   His main ally was Red Hugh O'Donnell.   Hugh's greatest victory took place against Sir Henry Bagenal, his brother-in-law and most ardent enemy, whose sister Mabel Bagenal he had married as his third wife in 1591.   Henry Bagenal lost nearly 2,000 men at this Battle of the Yellow Ford (1598) at which he himself was killed.

Victories at the pass of the Plumes, Glenmalure and at the Battle of the Curlews resulted in the opposing English commander, the Earl of Essex, being recalled to London where Elizabeth I had him beheaded as a consequence of the losses suffered against O'Neill.

Soon all was to be lost.   A new force consisting of 20,000 men arrived in Ireland under the command of Lord Mountjoy.   Mountjoy isolated Hugh O'Neill's allies and eventually defeated him at the battle of Kinsale in 1601. Hugh returned to Ulster and in 1603 renounced the title " O'Neill " and once again became Earl of Tyrone.

All his vassals were set free.   In September 1607, in an event known as " The Flight of the Earls ", he fled Ireland for Europe with ninety-nine others in such a hurry that he left behind his illegitimate son, Con.   The King of Italy, Paul V, invited him to Rome.   When he arrived he was given a private audience with the Pope who granted him a pension of 100 crowns a month and a house. The King of Spain granted him a monthly pension of 400 ducats. His ruined castle at Dungannon is illustrated in a seventeenth century map.

In a 1614 Inquisition in Co. Tyrone, O'Neill's lands were seized. Some of the commissioners on this Inquisition were clansmen including Turlagh McArt of Tempartlan, Con Boy McDonnell of Altedisart, Neile McArt of Inishe, Phelim McDonnell of Colenoran and Art Oge McDonnell of Aghinkean.   Known as " Illustrissimus princeps Hugo O'Nellus " on the continent of Europe, he died of a fever in Rome in 1616 and was buried in San Pietro.

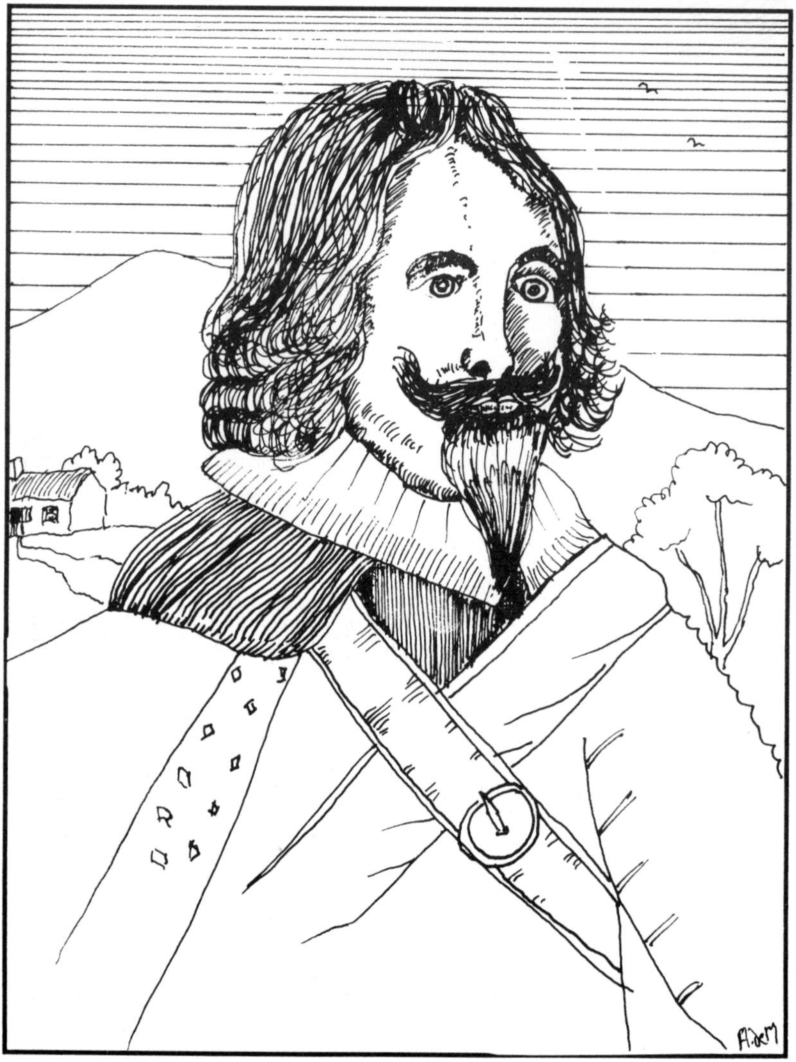

Sir Phelim O'Neill.

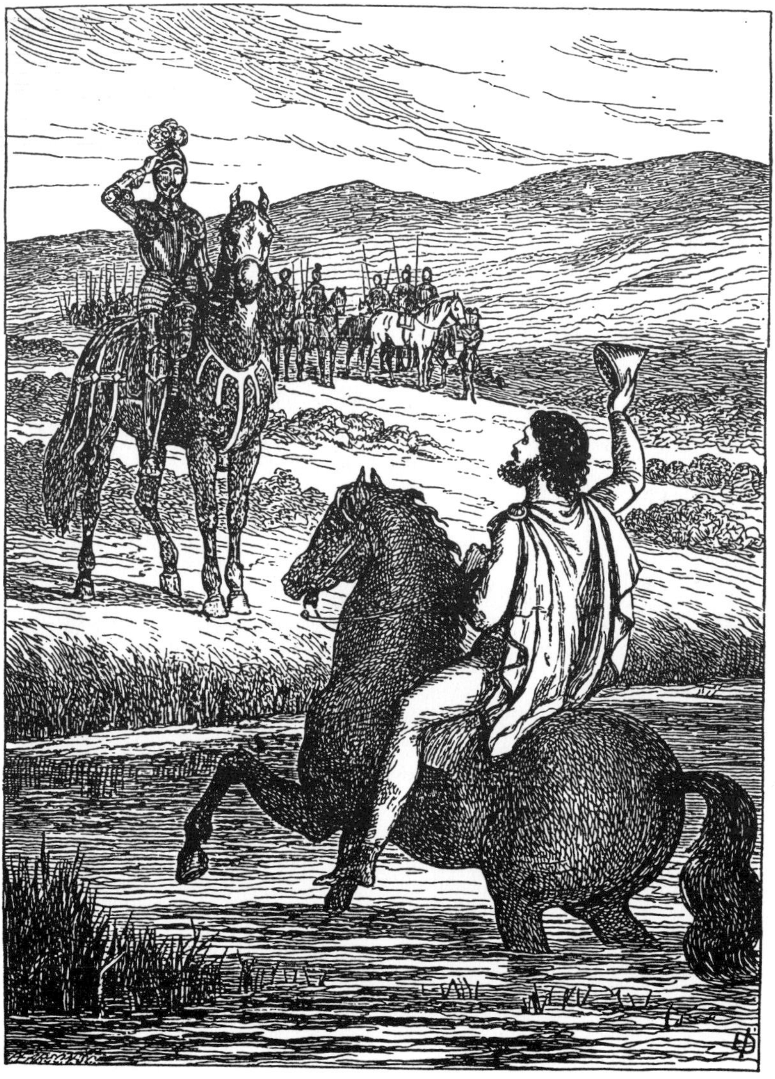

O'Neill and Essex.

Eoghan Rua O'Neill

Born in 1599, Eoghan Rua (Owen Roe) O'Neill was the son of Art and grandson of Matthew, Baron of Dungannon. His campaign in Ireland was born out of an effort by English puritans and Scottish presbyterians to oust the Gaelic Irish from their homes and lands in Ulster. Sir Phelim O'Neill had been readying himself to go to Catalonia with an Irish force when it was learned that General Leslie had landed a large army in Ulster. He changed his plans and prepared to oppose the invading army. He soon attacked Charlemont, while Con Magennis attacked Newry. A proposed foray on Dublin was betrayed. It was then decided to involve Eoghan Rua. The Abbot of Clunes, Abbot Connally, was sent with a message to Flanders where Eoghan was serving the Spanish forces in the "30 years war". Known to the Spanish, he was known as Don Eugenio, in 1642 Eoghan arrived at Lough Swilly on a ship called the "Francis" which was loaded with arms and men for the coming fight. In the same year, the Supreme Council of the Confederation of Catholics met for the first time and Eoghan Rua was made General of Ulster. His most famous victory came with his defeat of Monroe at the Battle of Benburb ten years later. It has been estimated that Monroe lost 3,000 men, four field pieces and twenty "colours" during this battle. After his victory, Eoghan Rua headed towards Tanderagee to take advantage of the confusion in the enemy ranks. But he was ordered to turn south by the Papal Nuncio who was connected to the Confederation of Catholics. Thereafter the war was gradually lost.

Henry McTully O'Neill, who fought with Eoghan Rua, related at a later date that "a pair of leather russet boots" which were sent to Eoghan Rua as a "present" by a gentleman of "the Plunketts from the county of Louth" had been deliberately poisoned in an effort to kill Eoghan. Further sources suggest that he died of complications brought on by gout and by the severe winter campaign of 1648. He had written a letter to Sir Nicholas Plunkett on the 25th September, 1649, which certainly suggests that he was suffering from sickness.

"...had I know of your coming heither already I would have made more expedition. Although the disposition of my body could not hitherto get me there unto by reason of a fit of sickness I took in my knee, which now (God be praised) begins to mend."

Eoghan Rua O'Neill died at the O'Reilly Castle on an island in Lough Oughter in County Cavan on the 6th November, 1649.

The Francis at Lough Swilly

Colonel Sir Daniel O'Neill

Born in around 1612, Daniel O'Neill was the son of con Mac Neill O'Neill who possessed Upper Clanaboy and Ards together with other property in County Antrim. His annual income from this was said to be £12,000. Daniel, who became a Protestant, also had a brother, Con Og. O'Neill. Through intrigue, the income he received from his father's property was reduced to £160 a year. In 1636 he served at the Seige of Breda. He supported the Royalist cause and used the pseudonym "Louis Lanois" in his correspondence with the forces in Ireland. He was later arrested and confined to the Tower of London but, in 1642, escaped dressed as a woman. He served as a Major in Colonel Osborne's regiment during the English Civil War. He fought at Gloucester and then at Newbury the following year. He was to have been sent to Ireland to raise an army of 10,000 for the fight in England but his enemies conspired. Just as he was about to set out on his mission, he was made the English King's "Groom of the Bedchamber".

Daniel fought at Marston Moor in 1644 and at Naseby the year after. In Ireland, he was nearly made General of the Army on the death of Eoghan Rua O'Neill, but the Papal representatives disagreed as he was still a Protestant and would not re-convert to Roman Catholicism.

When Charles II came to the English throne, Daniel's support of the royalist cause paid dividends. He was made Captain of the King's own Troop of Horse Guards. He became a Member of Parliament for St. Ives and acquired a large amount of land in London's St. James' Park and in Pall Mall. He was also the sole manufacturer of gunpowder for the Crown and Postmaster-General. From the fortune he had accumulated, he built Belsize House in Hampstead and a country house at Boughton-Malherbe in Kent. He also had patents on land in County Wexford because of a pension owed to him by the Crown. He was attempting to possess these lands when he died in 1664. Married, it is believed that he was childless and that no O'Neill acquired an interest in any part of his estate.

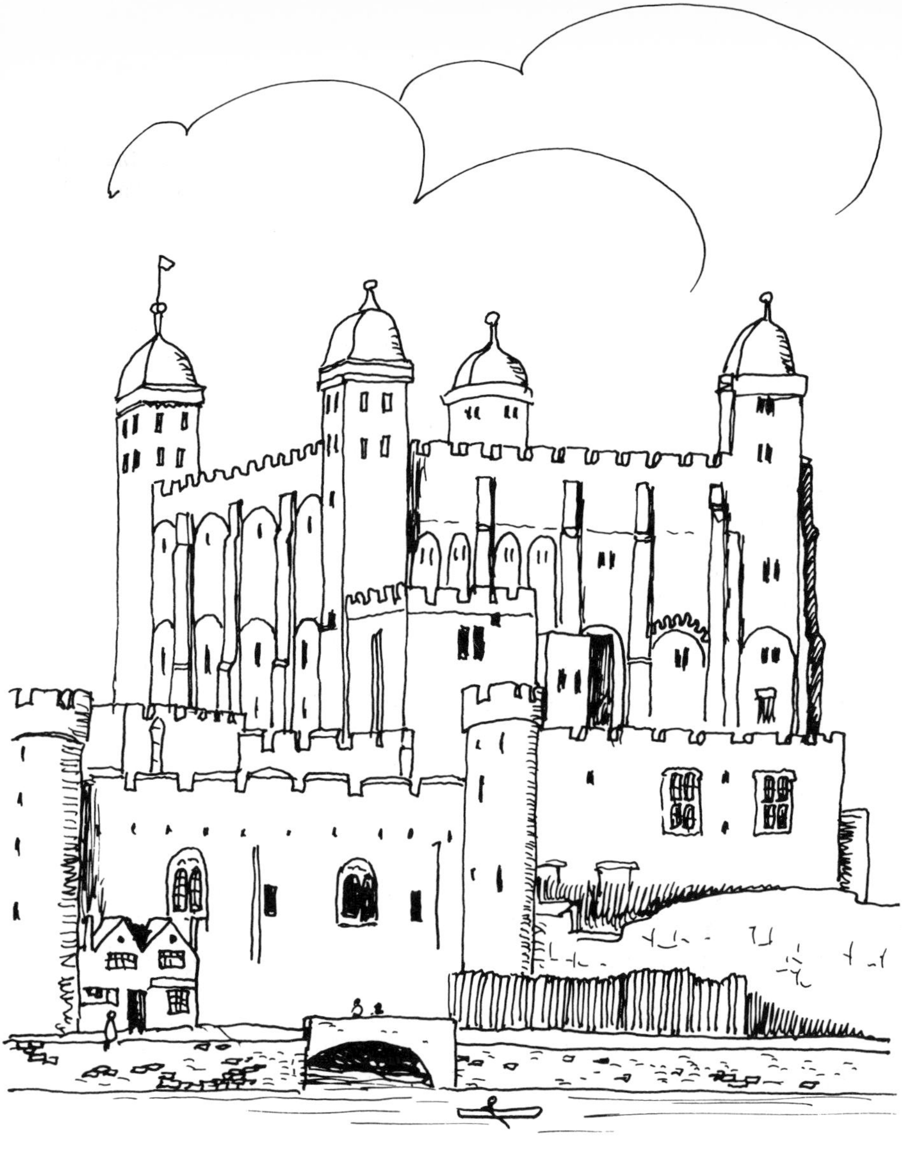

The Tower of London

Sir Niall O'Neill

Niall, sometimes refered to as Neill, O'Neill, was born in 1658. He was a son of Sir Henry O'Neill of Killelagh who was descended from Hugh O'Neill, Lord of Kilultagh in Clanaboy. Sir Henry O'Neill was knighted in 1666. Twenty years later, his son Niall raised a regiment of Dragoons for James II. He married Lady Frances Molyneux, the daughter of the Third Viscount Molyneux. His sister, Rose, married Captain Con O'Neill of the Fews.

During the war in Ireland between James II and William III, Sir Niall O'Neill served at the seige of Derry and was involved in a skirmish at Hacketstown in County Meath. He was also Lord Lieutenant of Armagh. At the Battle of the Boyne he was ordered to take his Dragoons and guard the ford at Rosnaree, an area close to the Slane bridge. He was confronted by Schomberg's choicest troops and was soon overcome. He received a wound to his thigh during the fracas. Niall was taken to Waterford where, it is said, he died soon after, on the 8th July, 1690, through the negligence of his surgeons. He was thirty two years old.

Niall O'Neill's brother, Sir Daniel O'Neill, was to have inherited his estates but, it is recorded, Niall was attainted and his property had been confiscated in 1691. Niall's wife Frances is supposed to have regained the land in 1700.

After his death, Niall's wife and five daughters, Rosa, Frances, Anne, Mary and Elizabeth retired to their grandmother's relatives at Carton in County Kildare. Sir Niall's father had married Eleanor Talbot, the daughter of Sir William Talbot of Carton. Rosa later married Nicholas Wogan of Rathcoffey and Anne married John Segrave of Cabra in County Dublin.

Sir Niall O'Neill is buried in the ruined Franciscan Abbey in Waterford city. An impressive portrait of him, done by John Michael Wright in 1680, is part of the portrait collection of the Tate Gallery in London.

Sir Niall O'Neill

Two O'Neill Musicians

Arthur O'Neill, born at Drumnaslad near Dungannon in County Tyrone in 1734 was the last of the wandering bards and a famous 18th century Irish harper. He was one of the O'Neills of Kinaird (Caledon) which was once the home of an important branch of the Clan. Arthur was blind by the age of two. There was a tradition that harping was reserved as a profession for blind sons of reduced Gaelic-Irish gentlemen. Arthur was instructed by Owen Keenan, another blind harpist . At fifteen, he set out on his career as an itinerant harper. He played mostly for old Irish families. When the Irish Harp Society was formed in Belfast, he became their resident master. Arthur was intensely proud of his O'Neill heritage and was known to have had silver buttons on his coat which depicted the "red hand" of the O'Neills. One of his most favourite harps was destroyed when his family home was set alight by Orangemen. Another harp which belonged to him is now in the Ulster museum. One biographical source states that he died in 1818 when he was eighty-five but another indicates that his death occurred two years later near Maydown in County Armagh. In any case he is buried in an unmarked grave in Eglish graveyard, three miles from Dungannon in County Tyrone.

Another O'Neill who contributed greatly to Irish traditional music was Captain Francis O'Neill. He was born at Bantry, County Cork, in 1849. He enlisted in the mercantile navy at an early age and served in the Mediterranean and on the Black Sea. He became an assistant steward on a ship called the Emerald Isle. He was once ship-wrecked off Baker Island while serving aboard the Minnehaha. His job enabled him to reach the United States of America. He settled there and undertook many different jobs until, in 1873, he joined the Chicago police force. After doing well in a Civil Service examination for the police, he became a Captain and was in 1901 made General Superintendent by the Mayor of Chicago. During this time, he had a great interest in traditional Irish music and on his retirement, spent twenty years until 1922 compiling many selections. He even used his own money to publish them. All of these publications are on sale in most Irish music shops. "The Music of Ireland", "The Dance Music of Ireland", "Irish Folk Music", Irish Minstrels and Musicians" and "Waifs and Strays of Irish Melody" are just some titles he published. Captain Francis O'Neill died in 1936. He left his collection to the University of Notre Dame, the famous North American Roman Catholic University.

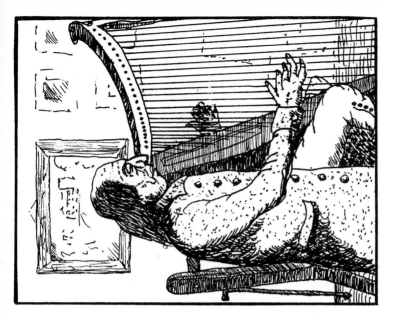

Arthur O'Neill

Captain Francis O'Neill

Inspector General John O'Neill

John O'Neill was born near Clontibret in County Monaghan in 1834. He emigrated to Elizabeth, New Jersey in the United States of America, where his mother was still living fourteen years later. During his early years in
the United States he worked as a shop clerk, a travelling salesman and was the proprietor of a Roman Catholic bookshop in Richmond. In 1857 he changed careers and joined the second United States Dragoons for the Morman War. For some reason, apparently not due to cowardice, he deserted from the army during this war and went to California where he served as a Sergeant in the First Cavalry during the American Civil War. At a later date, he joined the 5th Indiana Cavalry as a Second Lieutenant before being promoted to First Lieutenant. In 1846 he became Captain of the 17th United States Coloured Infantry but he left after a few months.

After this period of military activity he became involved with the Fenian Brotherhood in America. He was involved in leading 600 men across the Niagra River for an invasion on Fort Erie in Canada, one of a few "invasions" concocted by Fenians around this period. After becoming Inspector General of the Irish Republican Army in the U.S.A. in 1866, he once again led a raid across the Canadian border and attacked Eccles Hill and Pembina in Hudson Bay.

His interest in the Fenian Brotherhood diminished over time and he became involved in land speculation in Holt county, Nebraska. He encouraged Irish emigrants to settle there. Today, the main town in Holt county is called "O'NEILL", no doubt after its founder John O'Neill who died in Nebraska in 1878.

Eugene O'Neill

Nobel prizewinning playwright Eugene O'Neill was born in 1888. His father, James O'Neill, an actor born at Thomastown, County Kilkenny in 1864, was brought to America when he was eight. He played "The Count of Monte Cristo", 6,000 times. Eugene's mother, Ella Quinlan, was born in Cincinnati of Irish descent. She became addicted to morphine after being prescribed it following a difficult birth. Eugene spent his boyhood in New London, Connecticut.

His first marriage took place in 1909 to Kathleen Jenkins and he had one son by her called Eugene O'Neill junior who committed suicide. He divorced Kathleen in 1912, during which time he went to sea. His first trip was a 65 day journey to Buenos Aires, Argentina, on a Norwegian freighter.

Six years later Eugene was back in America where he married Agnes Boulton by whom he had Shane (b. 1920) and Oonagh (b. 1925). Shane suffered from alcoholism while Oonagh married Charlie Chaplin in 1943; when she was eighteen. Her father never forgave her; the reason is not known. Oonagh remained with Chaplin until his death and had several children including Geraldine Chaplin, the American actress. After his marriage to Carlotta Monterey in Paris in 1929, he stayed in France where he rented the Chateau de Plessis near Tours.

"The Iceman Cometh" was the last play Eugene O'Neill offered to the theatre in 1946 and by this time he had won the Nobel Prize for Literature. One of his most famous plays did not come to light until 1955. This was "A Long Days Journey into Night", an autobiographical work, about his own family life and his mother's morphine addiction. It was seen for the first time at the Royal Dramatic Theatre of Stockholm on 18th February, 1955. Eugene O'Neill was a prolific writer and actually destroyed his first eleven plays.

Amongst the plays he wrote were: "The Ancient Mariner" 1923, "Beyond the Horizon" 1917 - 18, "The Long Voyage Home" 1916 - 17, and "Strange Interlude" 1926 - 27.

Laurence O'Neill, T.D., Senator and Lord Mayor

Laurence O'Neill was born in Dublin in 1874. His father, John, was a corn factor with an address at 18 King's Inn Street. There is no record of John prior to 1867. At the turn of the century the family business moved into Smithfield Market, Dublin, where the company occupied itself as corn, hay and potato factors. They also operated a small mill. In 1911 Laurence was elected to Dublin City Council as a member for the Rotunda Ward. Six years later, he was elected Lord Mayor of Dublin and served seven consecutive terms of office until 1924. This was a record only surpassed by Alfie Byrne who was later to serve nine. O'Neill was known to be an honest negotiator and helped avert various strikes during his terms as Lord Mayor. There was no City Council between 1924 and 1930 but in 1930, at its restoration , Laurence was re-elected to and continued to serve as a Councillor until 1936. He also served as T.D. (Member of the Irish Parliament or Dail) for mid-Dublin from 1922 to 1925 and as a member of the Senate of the Irish Free State from 1929 to 1936.

Laurence O'Neill retired from politics in 1936. He had two children, John and Annie, by his wife Annie who died in January 1924. The family lived at Bridge House, Portmarnock, to the north of Dublin, until his death in 1943. Laurence bequeathed his interest as "salesman in the corporation market" to his son John in his Will.

He is buried at St. Marnock's cemetery, Portmarnock, where an impressive Celtic Cross marks his grave.

His family may be that of the O'Neills of Magh da Chonn.

Johnson (O'Neill) of New York

Thomas Mac Shane, son of John O'Neill and of Frances Fay, anglicised his name.   His son changed the surname yet again, to "Johnson". William Johnson had a grandson, William, who went to North America and became Colonel-in-Chief of the Sioux Nations in 1744 and, bearing the rank of Major General, defeated the French at Lake George in 1755.   For his services he was created a Baronet of New York.   Sir John Johnson was his son and the 2nd Baronet.   He was knighted in 1765.   He lived at Mount Johnson at Monreal in Canada.

Another of these Johnsons, Alexander Adair, was Captain of the New Zealand Expeditionary Force in Palestine.   He died in 1927 at the age of fifty-four.

The Escutcheon of this family is very similar to that of the other O'Neills, except that the mottoes differ.   The Johnson ones are "nec Aspera Terrent" and "Deo Regique Debeo".

These johnsons are descended from "O'Neills of the Fews" who were once transplanted to Mayo and Leitrim.

Their genealogy is recorded in Burke's Peerage and Baronetage.

Leac na Ri, The O'Neill Inauguration Stone at Tullaghoge

Terence O'Neill, Lord O'Neill of the Maine

Terence Marne O'Neill was born in London in 1914. His father was Captain Arthur O'Neill, a Member of Parliament for mid Antrim at Westminster, who died in the First World War.   In his autobiography Terence indicated regretfully, though proud to use the O'Neill surname, that in the male line he was a Chichester: "unfortunately and for the record, we are only descended from this ancient lineage, (the O'Neills) through the female line". His great grandfather, Sir William Chichester-O'Neill, inherited the O'Neill estates in 1868. He was the uncle of Raymond, Lord O'Neill of Shane's Castle.

In 1944, Terence O'Neill married Jean Whitaker.   He joined the Second Battalion, Irish Guards in 1940 having been commissioned Captain during the Second War.   His brother Brian, Adjutant of the First Battalion of the same regiment, was killed in Norway at the start of the war. Terence represented the constituency of Bannside for twenty-four years from 1946.   He became Prime Minister of Northern Ireland on the 25th March, 1963 and defeated the Reverend Ian Paisley in 1969. His moderate Unionism led to meetings and return meetings with Taoisigh Sean Lemass and Jack Lynch and with President de Valera.   He always considered his Gaelic-Irish and Anglo-Irish background to be beneficial to solving the ethnic and religious divide in Northern Ireland.

His ambition seems to have been the "Ulsterisation" of the six counties, under United Kingdom administration, with the consent of the Nationalists and the Unionists. He imagined that this would be followed by a breaking up of the United Kingdom into federal areas with their own parliaments. He foresaw that the Republic of Ireland could be more closely involved with a coalition of parliaments of the British Isles.   Another of his asperations was that there would eventually be a uniting of the English speaking peoples of the world.   He feared therefore that Britain, as a member of the European Community, would be isolated from this movement which he predicted would occur at the end of the century.   This portrayed an anti-European Community stance which possibly would not have pleased his cousin Sir Con O'Neill who negotiated Britain's entry into the Organisation.   He resigned as Prime Minister in 1969.

Terence O'Neill was made a life peer and adopted the name of a County Antrim river for his title, Lord O'Neill of the Maine. He died in 1990.

Terence, Lord O'Neill of the Maine

Ua Neill Mor, Don Carlos, Chief of his Name

The present "O'NEILL MOR" is Don Carlos O'Neill of Seville in Spain. He is also the 12th Marques de la Granja, the 4th Marques del Norte and the Conde de Banajiar.   His family is descended from Aodh O Neill, the second son of Eoghan O Neill, "THE O'NEILL", who died in 1465.   Aodh's descendants settled in County Armagh and became known as "The O'Neills of the Fews", presumably after the mountain range in that county. One family member, Sir Turlough Mac Henry O'Neill, was transplanted to the Counties Mayo and Leitrim area by Cromwell during the 17th century. The O'Neills of Seville are also descended from him.   The first to be born in Spain was Niall (1734), son of "Red" Henry, the grandson of Neill O'Neill of Cloon in County Leitrim. Tulio (born in 1743), a brother of Niall, married Catherine O'Keef Weler, and from him descends the present Marques de la Granja. Another brother was Arturo who lived between 1736 and 1814. He became Adjutant Major of the Hibernia regiment in Spain, Governor of Pensacola and Merida (c. 1792), and a member of the Supreme Council of War in 1802.   In 1805 he was created Marques del Norte by Carlos IV, King of Spain.   The title then passed to Tulio's son, another Tulio (1785-1855). This Tulio married Manuela de Castilla, a direct descendant of the famous Spanish King, Don Pedro de Castilla.   As a result of this marriage their son, Juan Antonio Luis O'Neill, inherted the titles of Marques de la Granja, Marques de Caltojar, Marques de Valdeosera and Conde de Benagiar.

Don Carlos O'Neill is recognised as the "O'NEILL MOR" by the Chief Herald of Ireland.   It is possible that he, or his son, will officially take up the title at the next O'Neill Clan Rally to be held during the summer of 1991. The photograph opposite, which was provided by Don Carlos, shows "ARTHOS O NEILL, Apostol de la Nueva, Escocia" who was said to have been killed during the crusades, in around 1282.   The O'Neill family tree was also kindly provided by Don Carlos.

BEATO
P. F.
ARTHŐS ONELL,
APOSTOL D LA NVEVA
ESCOCIA.

Art O'Neill - Martyred during Crusades 1282
(Convent of the Trinitarios Calzados de Madrid)

Ua Neill Buidhe, Hugo O'Neill, Chief of his Name

Hugo is the present "O'Neill of Clann Aodha Buidhe". He was born in 1939 in Lisbon. He is married to Rosa Maria, granddaughter of the Marques de Valencia, Premier Marquis of Portugal. They have three daughters, Luiza, Catarina and Maria-Ana Empis and one son Jorge who was born in 1970. Hugo O'Neill is a stockbroker. Jorge O'Neill, his father, inherited the title from a previous Hugo, he in turn having inherited from another Jorge O'Neill who was the first O'Neill of Portugal to hold it. In 1901, Augusta Eugene Valentine O'Neill de Tyrone of the O'Neills of Martinique made an agreement with the O'Neills of Portugal. These French O'Neills had become extinct in the male line and so she passed the title to the Portuguese, a move that the O'Neills of Paris did not receive kindly. Jorge, born in 1848, was known as Most Serene Prince and Count of Tyrone and Clanaboy. Hugo Joseph O'Neill, born twenty-six years later, was the next to hold the title. His son Jorge, born in 1908, was inaugurated as "O'Neill of Clann Aodha Buidhe" at Shane's Castle in 1982 when he was seventy-three. These O'Neills are descended in the female line from many Spanish and French Kings. Hugo's father was an industrialist and before his death he ran the family company which had over a thousand employees.

The pedigree of this family is written on parchment in Latin and dates to 1756. They are descended from Muircheartach, Prince of Clanaboy (1548-1552). One of their most famous descendants was Felim O'Neill, who was killed at Malplaquet in 1709. This was an appropriate end for a soldier who had fought at Derry, the Boyne and at Aughrim. After the Treaty of Limerick, he served the Irish Brigades in France. His son was Constantine whose son, Shane, was the first O'Neill to stay permanently in Lisbon. Shane's son Charles was visited by King John VI of Portugal at his house near Setubal. His son, Jose-Maria O'Neill, was Denmark's Consul General in Lisbon and his son, Jorge Torlades O'Neill, born in 1817, was a friend of Hans Christian Andersen with whom he frequently corresponded. He was also a Knight of the Rose of Brazil.

Hugo O'Neill is no stranger to Ireland and appeared on Bibi Baskin's R.T.E. Television show in 1990.

Hugo Ua Neill Buidhe and Family.

The O'Neills of Uibh Eoghain Fhinn

The Uibh Eoghain Fhinn is situated between Carrick-on-Suir and Clonmel, just south of Slievenaman in County Tipperary. The founder of these O'Neills was Conn, son of King Muircheartach of Cineal Eoghain, who was killed in 1160.   Conn O'Neill was instrumental in assisting Turlough O'Brien to recover the Kingdom of Thomond.   As a result the O'Briens have Conn territory which was originally somewhat larger than that mentioned above.   Conn married Albina who was a daughter of Reginald, the Norse King of Waterford. These O'Neills became known as "Lords of Ivowen", which is an anglicisation of Uibh Eoghain Fhinn. As late as the 17th century, they still considered the O'Neills of Ulster as their "kinsmen".

One of these O'Neills, "John Neale", was mentioned in the Ormond Deeds of 1516. He was "Thomas Neyll, Lord of the greater part of Carrick". Art FitzJohn O'Neill, who rented land to Sir James Clere, the Dean of Kilkenny, in or around 1543 was another, these O'Neills had their lands confiscated during the Cromwellian period.   Written in Irish their history has recently been published "Gleann an Oir" was written and researched by Colonel Eoghan O Neill who is the main representative of the O'Neills of Uibh Eoghain Fhinn.

The following is a simplified family tree of the O'Neills of Uibh Eoghain Fhinn.

CONN + ALBINA, circa 1150
SEAN, circa 1460 - 1530
ART, circa 1530
BRIAN, 1560
CONN, circa 1560 - 1629
AODH BUI, circa 1590 - circa 1662
CONN, 1635 - 1725
SEANA - SHEAN, circa 1670 - circa 1745
SEAN OG, 1697 - 1780
RISTEARD, 1745 - 1811
AODH, 1775 - 1847
FEIDHLIM, 1810 - 1901
AND (HIS CHILDREN)
CONN, AODH, EOGHAN AND SIOBHAN

Ballyneale Castle, situated between Sleivenaman and the river Suir, is about four kilometrers to the west north west of Carrick on Suir town. The castle, built in the early seventeenth century, was a rectangular three storey gentleman's residence with a circular tower at each of two opposite corners. Conn O'Neill, who died in 1629 aged sixty-nine, was buried in a tomb in the nearby Kilmurry graveyard. Dr. Patrick Power, in his book "Carrick on Suir and its People", points out that the carvings on the sides of the tomb which depict the instruments of the Passion of Christ, "seem so like the woodcuts in a copy of the 'Little Office of the Blessed Virgin', which was published in Antwerp in 1630, that the stone-carver may have had the book with him as he worked". Conn was succeeded by his son Aodh Buidh O'Neill.

In 1774, a Cornelius Neal was Church of Ireland Churchwarden at St. Mary's Clonmel. Samuel Neale, of Christianstown, Co. Kildare, who died in 1845 may well also have been a member of the Ballyneale Castle family.

The O'Neills of Magh da Chonn

It is proposed that research into this family by the author, including the compilation of over 1,500 names from the 16th century to the beginning of the 20th, will be published in 1991 by the Irish Heritage Association titled "The O'Neills of Leinster".

While some sources declare that the O'Neills of Magh de Chonn are of Ulster descent, it is almost certain that they are descended from Nath I, son of Crimthann who was King of Leinster for forty years in the 5th century. These O'Neills are a sept of the Ui Chennselaig along with the Kavanaghs, MacMorroughs, Murphys and Kinsellas. The surname was used in the 10th century by Domnall Ua Neill who was beheaded fighting the Norsemen. Their genealogy from Cathair Mar, a second century King of Ireland, until the 12th century is extensive but it is practically non existant from then to the beginning of the 16th century except for several references to them in poems and Annals. Their later genealogy has been reconstructed from the FIANTS of Edward VI and Elizabeth I, when nearly fifty Carlow O'Neills are mentioned as being pardoned after they had revolted, agains the English, under the command of the Kavanaghs. The chief of these O'Neills mainly dispersed into Wicklow and Wexford. A descendant of Donagh could be "chief" of the O'Neills of Magh da Chonn and could, without doubt, be entitled to call himself "UA NEILL a Magh da Chonn ", a title which goes back to the 10th century.

These O'Neills have no Coat of Arms and it would be incorrect for any O'Neill descended from them to use the Coats of Arms of the O'Neills of Ulster or Uibh Eoghain Fhinn.

O'Neills - Landowners Carlow / Wexford

Constantine Neal, a Commonwealth soldier who died in 1692, was in around 1666 awarded large tracts of land in Co. Wexford, mainly in the barony of Forth, the East Ward of Wexford town, and the town of New Ross of which he was a Sheriff and Freeman. In a manuscript in Marshes Library, Dublin, concerning the Baltinglass and O'Neal families, is stated that he was "descended from the Kings of Ireland", which denotes Ulster descent. Unfortunately this cannot be determined as Constantine is not mentioned in any contemporary conflagrations. He may have been one of the English 'Neales' who are distantly related to the Ulster Ui Neill. Constantine's only son Benjamin, of Mount Neal near Kilmurry on the Carlow-Kildare border, was a doctor of Theology and chaplain with King William of Orange at the Battle of the Boyne. He also served the Duke of Ormond. For his bravery at the battle, he was awarded land in Co. Carlow and later was nominated as Archdeacon of Leighlin. Made a Freeman of the town of New Ross in 1703, Benjamin married Hannah, daughter of Sir Joshua Paul, whose family had property in Carlow and Dublin. A daughter, Martha O'Neill, married John Stratford, the Earl of Aldeborough, whose family were later to hold the title "Lord Baltinglass". Their son, Edward, inherited the lands in Carlow and Kildare from Hannah O'Neill on her death in 1764 and his brother, Benjamin O'Neal Stratford, was Governor of Wicklow in 1778. Martha's sister Deborah eloped with John Bayly of Debsboro', Co. Tipperary, in 1718. After Bayly's death, she married again to Henry Prittie of Dunalley Castle. These O'Neills did not have any male heirs so the property ownership passed from the family name.

O'Neill Army Officers in the Service of France, Spain and of America.

1. Colonel Charles O'Neill of Derrynoose, Co. Armagh became Chef du Bureau de L'Infanterie au Ministre de la Guerre and Officer de la Legion d'Honneur, in France.

2. Colonel Gordon O'Neill, son of Sir Phelim of Kinard fought with the Irish Brigade, with the Regiment of Charlemont, in France.

3. General John O'Neill fought with the Regiment de Walsh in the Irish Legion, circa 1793, in France.

4. Sub. Lieutenant Henri Felix Jean O'Neill, fought with the Irish Legion, with the 7th Regiment de Cuirassiers, in France during Napoleon's time.

5. Count Jacques O'Neill de Tyrone, who died in 1839, also fought with the 7th Regiment de Cuirassiers.

6. Viscount Francois Henri O'Neill de Tyrone also fought with the Regiment de Cuirassiers.

7. The following O'Neills served in the Irish Regiments in Spain such as those of Limerick, Waterford, Hibernia and Irlanda.
   El Conde, circa 1705, Sub. Lieutenant Don Bernardo, Don Terencio, circa 1718, Captain Don Arturon, circa 1715, Super Captain Don Carlos, circa 1715, Colonel Brigadier Don Felix, circa 1760, Captain Don Eugenio, Circa 1768, Lieutenant Don Antonio, circa 1768, Sub Lieutenant Don Constantino, circa 1768, Sub Lieutenant Don Terencio, circa 1768, Sub. Lieutenant Don Terencio, circa 1777, Sub. Lieutenant Don Felix, circa 1777, Cadet Don Pedro, circa 1739, Cadet Don Enriquez, circa 1784.

8. Colonel Armand Marie O'Neill, of the Regiment de la Ligne is mentioned in the Annuaires de l'Armee Francaise in 1873-76

9. The following served with General Thomas Meagher as part of the Irish Brigade in the American War (1861-65):
   Captain B.S. O'Neill, Captain J.O. O'Neill, Captain John O'Neill, Colonel Thomas O'Neill and Major Joseph O'Neill who served in the 69th and 63rd New York Volunteers, 116 Pennsylvania Volunteers and the Battery, Irish Brigade.

10. Carlos Felix O'Neill, who died in Spain in 1791, was a Governor of Havannah, Cuba.

11. Captain Hugo O'Neill, of O'Donnell's Brigade, the son of Felix O'Neill and of Margaret Magines (MacGuiness) married Jane Bourke at the Church of Jacques du Haut, at Germain en Laye, Paris in May 1710.

O'Neill Surname Variations

Nail	O'Neall
Neil	O'Neile
Neal	Onyll
Neale	O'Neel
Neel	O'Neyll
Neill	Neilson
Neile	Nelson
Neall	Nihill
O'Nayle	Nihell
O'Neil	Nihil
O'Neale	Creagh
O'Neal	O'Nihill
O'Nele	

It is often reported that the name O'Neill means champion but it is basically the name of the grandfather of Domnall Ua Neill, King of Ireland, and Domnall Ua Neill of Magh da Chonn, both of whom lived in the 9th to 10th centuries. The Irish started using surnames in the 10th century. the Ulster O'Neills are named after Niall Glundubh (Black Knee) King of Ireland (916-919) and the O'Neills of Magh da Chonn are named after the lesser known Neill (Niall), mentioned in the Book of Leinster genealogies. These genealogies date back to the Book of Dub-da-lethe, A.D. 1050.

Other "O'Neills", for various reasons, parade under the surnames of Johnson, Paine and MacShane.

The Journal of the Royal Society of Antiquarians in Ireland Volume XIII, gives the genealogy of the "O'Neills" of Thomond and states that they are descended from "Carthin Find" (circa 439) and get their name from "Congal a quo O'Neoghan".

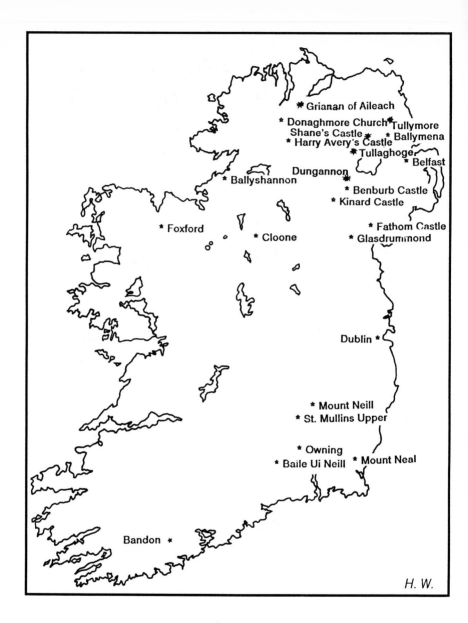

* Grianan of Aileach
* Donaghmore Church * Tullymore
Shane's Castle * * Ballymena
* Harry Avery's Castle
* Tullaghoge
* Belfast
Dungannon
* Ballyshannon *
* Benburb Castle
* Kinard Castle
* Foxford
* Fathom Castle
* Cloone
* Glasdrummond

Dublin *

* Mount Neill
* St. Mullins Upper

* Owning
* Baile Ui Neill * Mount Neal

Bandon *

H. W.

Ireland. Significant O'Neill Places.

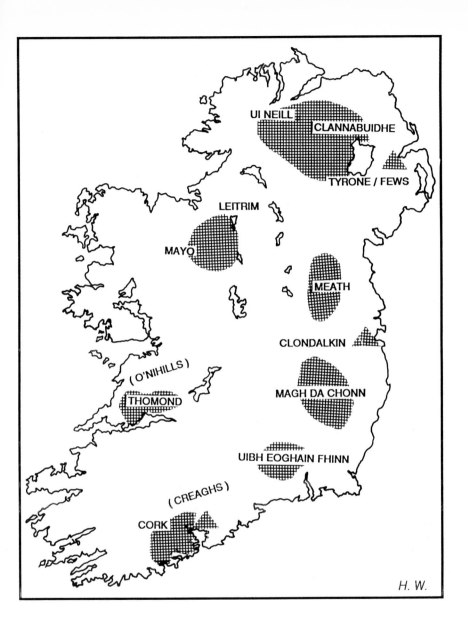

Ireland. Significant O'Neill Areas.

Some O'Neill Places

BALLYNASAGGERT: This monastery was founded by Conn O'Neill, c.1489.

BELSIZE HOUSE: A London residence built for Colonel Sir Daniel O'Neill in the seventeenth century.

BENBURB CASTLE: The present plantation castle built by Sir Richard Wingfield is on the site of an earlier castle belonging to Sir Shane O'Neill in 1556.

BONE SUCCESSO CONVENT: Lisbon. The Portuguese convent where two daughters of John O'Neill became successively prioresses and where they were buried.

CAISLEANN UI NEILL: Co. Tipperary. Situated in Ballyneill, this castle which is now a ruin, belonged to the Ui Neill of Uibh Eoghain Fhinn.

CALEDON CASTLE: also Kinard. A castle here, built by Turlough O'Neill in 1619 replaced an earlier building. After destruction following the battle of Benburb, this was again replaced.

CARRICKFERGUS CASTLE: Co. Antrim. This norman castle was not built by O'Neills but Niall Mor O'Neill occupied it sometime before 1512.

CASTLEREAGH: Belfast. This site was the former County Antrim inauguration site of the O'Neills of Clann Aodha Buidhe. The inauguration chair is now in the Ulster museum.

CLANABOY: Northern Ireland. From Tir Owen, the Land of Owen (O'Neill). A large 1211 square mile County west of Lough Neagh with Omagh as its chief town.

CLEGGAN LODGE: Ballymena. The two storey once thatched home of the Lords Rathcavan in Co. Antrim.

CONVENT OF CARRICKFERGUS: Co. Antrim. Built by Niall Mor O'Neill, circa 1497.

CREGGAN CHURCH: Co. Armagh. This church was built by the O'Neills of Glasdrummond, circa 1500. A vault containing O'Neill skeletons was recently discovered there. This vault has been restored.

DONAGHMORE CHURCH: Castlefinn, Co. Donegal. Fifth century church founded by St. Patrick who was there befriended by Eoghan of Aileach.

DRUMDERG: This house belonged to the O'Neills of the Feeva, Co. Antrim in 1641.

DUNGANNON ABBEY: Co. Tyrone. In 1489, Con O'Neill founded a monastery for Tertiary Franciscans at Dungannon.

DUNGANNON CASTLE: Co. Tyrone. Built by Hugh O'Neill at the end of the sixteenth century. Destroyed by Mountjoy. In 1619 it was

described by Pynnar as being 120 feet square with four half bul
- warks with a number of stone and timber frame houses.

EDIFICIO LUSITANIA: Seville. The residence, in the Avenida de Portugal, of the Marques de la Granja.

FATHOM CASTLE: County Armagh. There used to be an O'Neill castle at Fathom, three miles south of Newry. It was built on the orders of Shane "The Proud" O'Neill circa 1563.

GLASDRUMMOND CASTLE: County Armagh. This castle once existed at Crossmaglen. It was built around 1450 after the O'Neills came south to this area, ousting the O'Callaghans, Murphys and Hanrat -tys. The O'Neills became chieftains of 10,000 acres.

GRIANAN OF AILEACH: see page 10.

MOUNT NEAL: Co. Wexford. The home of Benjamin Neale/O'Neale and later of his son-in-law, John, Earl of Aldborough. This house was destroyed by fire in 1799.

MOUNT NEILL: Co. Kilkenny. Situated in the Barony of Iverk. This was the home of a John O'Neill at the end of the 18th century. He was formerly an O'Neill of Uibh Eoghain Fhinn.

O'NEILL CASTLE AT KINARD: Kinard, now called Caledon, belonged to "Bryan na Murtough" O'Neill in the 16th century.

O'NEILL'S CASTLE, BELFAST:This castle belonged to Bryan mac Phelim O'Neill, Prince of Clann Aodha Buidhe, who was murdered by the Earl of Essex at a banquet in 1575.

O'NEILL'S CASTLE: Co. Antrim. This castle is now a ruin in the townland of Kerlish.

O'NEILL MANSION: Viscount and Baron John O'Neill of Shane's Castle lived at 9 Henrietta Street, Dublin, when attending Grattan's Parlia -ment in the 18th century.

PARK HILL: Ballyshannon. A modest, once thatched, two storey O'Neill house buillt in the mid 18th century.

QUINTAS DAS MACHADAS: Portugal. The country residence of the Portuguese O'Neills. They also have a town house, Rua da Junqueira 10, in Lisbon and once owned a large mansion "Torre de Sao Patricio" (Tower of St. Patrick) which is now a museum.

ROUGHAN CASTLE: Newmills. An impressive 17th century strong house built by Sir Andrew Stewart but shortly afterwards occupied by Sir Phelim O'Neill who was executed in 1653 after his rebellion.

ST. PETER'S PRO CATHEDRAL: Belfast. Completed by Architect John O'Neill in 1866 and by which he established his reputation.

SHANE'S CASTLE: Co. Antrim. Otherwise known as Edenduffcarrick, it is thought to have been built in the 12th century. Destroyed by fire

in 1816. The present structure close by was built in the 19th century.
TULLYMORE LODGE: Co. Antrim. Situated in Broughshane, this two storey house with its interesting row of chimneys was the dower house of the O'Neills of Shane's Castle until the 1930s. It was built by Charles O'Neill who died in 1769.
TYRONE: Northern Ireland. From Tir Owen, the Land of Owen (O'Neill). A large 1211 square mile county west of Lough Neagh with Omagh as its chief town.

Miscellaneous

1   <u>American O'Neills</u>
In the United States of America, there are some 150,000 members of the O'Neill Clan. Most of them bear the names O'Neill, O'Neal or O'Neil in the foregoing order.

2   <u>Irish O'Neills</u>
There are 8,000 O'Neills in the Republic of Ireland and more than 3,500 in Northern Ireland, making a total of more than 11,500 clansmen in all Ireland.

3   <u>O'Neill Clan News</u>
This Belfast published journal features articles about various aspects of O'Neill heritage and matters of potential interest to readers. It also publishes a list of reader's queries.

4   <u>The Royal O'Neill Clann Society</u>
Based at Belfast, this society is administered by Mrs. Kathleen Neill, AUGRA at 162A, Kingsway, Dunmurray, Belfast BT17 9AD. (Telephone 0232 629595) and organised the inauguration of the late Jorge O'Neill of Portugal as The O'Neill of Clannabuidhe in 1982.

5   <u>1991 International Clan Gathering</u>
Commencing with an all-Ireland heritage tour from Shannon, this prestigious event is being attended by The O'Neill Mor, Don Carlos O'Neill, Marques de la Granja y Marques del Norte.

Major late 19th Century O'Neill Landowners

CREAGH, Arthur, 9 Steamfort, Mallow Co. Cork.   538 acres in Co. Cork.
150 acres in Co. Limerick.
CREAGH, Mrs. Barbara, Ennistymon.   78 acres in Co. Clare.
CREAGH, Brazier, Geo. W., Youghal.   473 acres in Co. Cork.
CREAGH, Cornelius, Dangan, Tulla.   6,004 acres in Co. Clare.
CREAGH, Mrs. Eliza, Creagh Cas.,Doneraile.   2,873 acres in Co. Cork.
CREAGH, Francis and John, Tarmons, Co. Kerry. 829 acres in Co.Kerry.
CREAGH, Gethin Arthur.   1,361 acres in Co. Cork.
CREAGH, John, Cork.   396 acres in Co. Cork.
CREAGH, John B. 9 Holles Street, Dublin.   173 acres in Co. Clare.
150 acres in Co. Limerick.

CREAGH, Kilner, Creagh Cas., Doneraile.   225 acres in Co. Cork.
CREAGH, M. Reps of, Doneraile.   734 acres in Co. Cork.
CREAGH, Mary, Carahan, Quin.   330 acres in Co. Clare.
CREAGH, Paul, Fairymount, Co. Limerick.   92 acres in Co. Limerick.
CREAGH, Philip William, Mitchelstown.   1,141 acres in Co. Cork.
CREAGH, Richard, England.   153 acres in Co. Cork.
CREAGH, Richard, Millbrook, Clonmel.   453 acres in Co. Tipperary.
CREAGH, Richard, G., c/o James Lane South Mall, Cork.
436 acres in Co. Cork.
CREAGH, Simon Pierce, Mt. Elva, Lisdoonvarna. 1,907 acres in Co. Clare.
CREAGH, William, Ballygarrett, Mallow.   1,124 acres in Co. Cork,
829 acres in Co. Kerry.
CREAGHE, Grace A., Hampstead, London.   354 acres in Co. Clare.
CREAGHE, . Capt. Jas., Army & Navy Club, London.
388 acres in Co. Clare.
NEALE, George, Coolrain, Mountrath. 75 acres + 428 acres in Co. Laois.
NEILL, Harriett, Reps of.   137 acres in Co. Kildare.
NEILL, Henry J. Rockport.   94 acres in Co. Down.
NEILL, Hugh, Killaroo, Streamstown.   82 acres in Co. Westmeath.
NEILL, James & John, Derrylacky, Mullinavat. 108 acres in Co. Kilkenny.
NEILL, Joseph, Christianstown, Kildare.   507 acres in Co. Kildare.
O'NEILL, The Right Hon. Lord, Shane's Castle, Antrim.
64,163 acres in Co. Antrim,
804 acres in Co. Tyrone.
O'NEILL, Anne, Derrymoyle, Laois.   101 acres in Co. Laois.
O'NEILL, Catherine.   1,106 acres in Co. Carlow.
O'NEILL, Francis, Reps of. Mount Pleasant, Strabane. 117 acres in Co.Tyrone.

O'NEILL, Henry, Portstewart. 83 acres in Co. Derry.
O'NEILL, Henry, Annsbrook, Lusk 134 acres in Co. Dublin.
O'NEILL, Henry, Shanballyduff, Thurles. 155 acres in Co. Tipperary.
O'NEILL, Major Henry. 351 acres in Co. Kildare.
O'NEILL, John, Londonderry. 83 acres in Co. Derry.
O'NEILL, John, Sarsfield's Court, Riverstown, Cork. 82 acres in Co. Cork.
O'NEILL, John. 313 acres in Co. Cork.
O'NEILL, Joseph, Annaghmore, Coalisland. 108 acres in Co. Tyrone.
O'NEILL, Mary, Kilmace, Screen. 593 acres in Co. Wexford.
O'NEILL, Owen, Urglin, Co. Carlow. 76 acres in Co. Carlow.
O'NEILL, Philip, Ballydaniel, Ballymacoda. 237 acres in Co. Cork.
O'NEILL, Robert, Glenmaroon, Chapelizod 143 acres in Co. Dublin.
O'NEILL, The Hon. Robert Thomas, Derrynoid Lodge, Draperstown,
4,844 acres in Co. Derry.
O'NEILL, Thomas, Creagh, Castledawson. 172 acres in Co. Derry.

Distribution Summary of 19tn Century O'Neill Lands.

	Acres		Acres
Co. Antrim	64243	Co. Kilkenny	189
Co. Armagh	99	Co. Laois	547
Co. Carlow	1247*	Co. Louth	130
Co. Clare	9307*	Co. Limerick	1268*
Co. Cork	9623*	Co. Offaly	169
Co. Derry	5327	Co. Tipperary	611*
Co. Donegal	17	Co. Tyrone	1113
Co. Down	196	Co. Waterford	16
Co. Dublin	382	Co. Westmeath	83
Co. Galway	4	Co. Wexford	597
Co. Kerry	1223*	Co. Wicklow	1
Co. Kildare	1013	* These Figures Include Creagh property.	

Scotland - Capt. W.J.S. O'Neill, 1275 acres in Ayreshire. Total in Scotland 1327 acres.
England - W. Neal, Somerset. 2170 acres . Total in England 2170.

Countless acress of lands leased to the O'Neill became their property in the late 19th and early 20th century land reforms.

A Short List of O'Neill Biography

Neal, Rev. Daniel. Author "History of the Puritans etc" (1732) and "History of New England" (1700) b. 1678 (London) d. 1743

Neal, John, American Lawyer, writer, Newspaper Editor and Lecturer b. 1793 (America) d. 1876

Neal, Patricia, U.S. Actress film star (A Face in the Crowd - 1957 etc.) b. 1926 (New York)

Neale, family. Emigrated from Ireland to America with Leonard Calvert in 1633. Settled Virginia.

Neale, Ven. Charles Sidney. Anglican Archdeacon in Brazil. b. c. 1890

Neale, Edward Vansittart, Lawyer, Pioneer Christian Socialist and Co-op founder. b. 1810 (Bath) d. 1892.

Neale, Rev. John Mason. Hymnologist whose collected hymns published 1914 b. 1818 (London) d. 1866.

Neel, Edmund, CIE (1890). Secretary Indian Public Works Department . b. 1841.

Neill, Alexander Sutherland. Educationalist and writer, Editor "New Era". b. 1883 (Scotland) d. 1973

Neill, Desmond Gorman, M.A., Academic Council Secretary, Q.U.B., Educator, author and administrator. b. 1913 (Madras)

Neill, Ivan, N. Ireland politician (leader of N. House of Commons 1964), building contractor, b. 1906

Neill, Rev. Ivan Delacherois, C.B., M.A., Chaplain to Queen Elizabeth II (1962-1966) b. 1912 (Cloughjordan).

Neill, Rt. Rev. John Robert Winder, Bishop of Tuam (1985)

Neill, Rt. Rev. Stephen Charles, D.D. Missionary author and Theologian. Bishop of Tirunelveli (India) b.1900 (Edinburgh) d.1984

Neill, Very Rev. William Benjamin Alan, Dean of Waterford (1986)

O'Neal, Ryan, U.S. Film and Television actor father of Tatum O'Neal b. 1941 (Los. Angeles)

O'Neale, Tatum, U.S. child actress and film star (Paper Moon etc.) b. 1963 (Los Angeles)

O'Neill, Most Rev. Aed, Bishop of Derry, c. 1316.

O'Neill, Most Rev. Alexander Henry, M.A., D.D., Archbishop of Fredericton (Canada) 1963-1971. b. c. 1908.

O'Neill, Cathal, Architect and University College, Dublin Lecturer, b.1930

O'Neill, Charles, M.B., Professor of Botany (Glasgow) and Nat. M.P. for South Armagh (1909) d. 1917

O'Neill, The Hon. Con Douglas Walter, G.C.M.G., Banker and E.C. negotiator for Britain's entry. b.1912.

O'Neill, Daniel Joseph, Ph.D., M.B., U.S. lecturer in Polymer Science and
    writer. b. 1942 (Boston)

O'Neill, Daniel, Selftaught figurative painter b. 1920 (Belfast) d. 1974
    (U.S.A.)

O'Neill, Denis, C.B, British Parliamentarian. b. 1908

O'Neill, Hon. Sir Desmond Henry, W. Australian Liberal M.P. and Minister
    for Housing (1974-1975), b. 1920

O'Neill, Donell, Grandson of King Niall and first to bear family name. d.
    919 A..D.

O'Neill, Eliza, Lady Beecher, Dublin and Covent Garden actress (m.
    William Beecher, M.P, for Mallow) b. 1791 (Drogheda) d.
1872 (Mallow)

O'Neill, Eugene, Canon of the Church of Armagh, c. 1495.

O'Neill, Eugene Gladstone, U.S. playwright.   Pulitzer and Nobel prize-
    winner b. 1888 (N. York), d. 1953.

O'Neill, Most Rev. Dr. Henry, R.C. Archbishop of Dromore, c. 1907

O'Neill, James, U.S. actor (Count of Monte Cristo, six thousand times)
    and father of Eugene O'Neill b. 1849 (Kilkenny) d. 1920

O'Neill, James Peter, M.B., M.R.C.P., Mercy Hospital Cork Consultant
    Physician. b. 1931

O'Neill, John, Cobbler and shoemaker, then London dramatist. b.1777
    (Cork) d. 1860.

O'Neill, John, General Manager, Killeshandra Group, Chairman Bord
    Bainne etc. b. 1912 (Cork)

O'Neill, John Carter, Physician to Queen Victoria. b. 1845.

O'Neill, John Joseph (Jonjo) National Hunt Champion Jockey and Gold
    Cup winner (Dawn Run). b. 1952 (Cork)

O'Neill, Major General John J. Silverston, C.B., Served Crimea, Lucknow
    etc. b. 1835.

O'Neill, Joseph Francis St. John, Cork County Registrar, Lawyer and
    Fine Gail supporter. b. 1916

O'Neill, Maire Treasa. Abbey Theatre and film actress. B. Galway

O'Neill, Margaret (Peggy), U.S. actress, m. Secretary of State John
    Eaton b. 1796 (Washington), d. 1879

O'Neill, Martin John, Labour M.P. for Clackmannan (1983) and Defence
    Spokesman (1984), Schoolmaster. b. 1945 (Scotland)

O'Neill, Maurice, Editor Ballymena Guardian (1971) b. 1938 (Ballymena)

O'Neill, Michael, Mid Ulster Republican M.P., (1951-55) and Contractor,
    b. 1909

O'Neill, Michael Anthony, Chairman, M.D., John Parson & son, etc., b.
    1940 (Dublin)

O'Neill, Most Rev. Michael Cornelius, O.B.E., R.C. Archbishop of Regina (Canada). b. 1898.

O'Neill, Rev. Nevil, M.A.,, C.I. Dean of Clogher (1981).

O'Neill, Niall, Prior of Disert Monastery, Connor Diocese, c. 1490.

O'Neill, Owen Roe, D.P.A., N. Manpower Service Director, Dept. of Labour b. 1917 (Limerick).

O'Neill, Patrick, U.S. Character actor, film star and restauranteur. b. 1927 (Florida).

O'Neill, Professor Patrick Geoffrey, Ph.D., London Univeristy lecturer on Japanese and author. b. 1924.

O'Neill, Patrick Joseph, Lawyer, Urban District Councillor and Fine Gael supporter. b. 1908 (Kildare).

O'Neill, Patrick Joseph, B.A., Lawyer, M.D., Belleek Pottery Ltd. (1954) b. 1921 (Dublin).

O'Neill, Lt. Col. Peter, C.B.S., National Executive Officer (1970), U.N. Middle East Force (1968-1969).

O'Neill, Sir Randall, Baronet, of Rush, Co. Dublin (Meath O'Neills), c. 1777.

O'Neill, Raymond Benedict, M.B., B.ch., V.C.E. lecturer in Forensic Medicine b. 1915 (Cork).

O'Neill, Raymond Joseph, LL.B., S.C., Lawyer, Governor of the Rotunda. b. 1912 (Dublin)

O'Neill, Robert James, C.M.G., British Diplomat and Under Secretary of State. b. 1932

O'Neill, Dr. Robert John, Australian Military Strategist and author. b. 1936 (Australia)

O'Neill, Seamus, M.A., Professor of Irish History and writer, b. Co. Down.

O'Neill, Sean, Cleric in Down Diocese, c. 1490.

O'Neill, Sonny. Reputedly fired the shot that killed Michael Collins in 1922. b. Co. Cork.

O'Neill, Tom, M.A., University linguistic lecturer in Australia, Editor and writer. b. 1942 (Scotland).

O'Neill, Thomas Philip (Tip), U.S. Democratic Senator and Speaker of the House (1970), Irish Citizen, b. 1912.

O'Neill, Count Thomas, Sailor and author. Helped Portuguese Royal Family escape from Napoleon, held at Bastille.

O'Neill, William Atkinson, Governor of Connecticut (1980) b. 1930.

O'Nial, John, Surgeon General and Principal Medical Officer, Nile Expeditionary Force (1884-1885). b. 1827.

O'Neills Mentioned in the Civil Survey
Co. Tyrone 1654 - 1656.

Neal McHenry O'Neale, Catholic	Derrgloran	50 acres
Phelemy Grom O'Neale, Catholic	Ballinderry	40 acres
Sir Philemy O'Neale, Catholic	Half of Aghelow	2190 acres
Torlagh McArt Og O'Neale, Catholic	Carnteall	520 acres
	Killissill	120 acres
	Clonfiekle	100 acres
	Donaghmore	200 acres
Cormick O'Neale (Deceased)	Clonfiekle	40 acres
Con Bui/Boy O'Neale	Donaghmore	100 acres
Bryan McArt O'Neale	Donaghmore	100 acres
Donell O'Neale	Donaghmore	80 acres
Catlin ni Neale	Donaghmore	40 acres

The Following Served in the
Irish House of Commons c. 1689

Ulster Members representing:-

Antrim	Cormuck O'Neile
Borough of Lisburn	Daniel O'Neile
Borough of Armagh	Constantine O'Neile
Borough of Killyleagh	Tool O'Neile of Dromankelly
Borough of Dungannon	Arthur O'Neile of Ballygawley
County Tyrone	Colonel Gordon O'Neile

Governors of Counties: Ulster.   1689.

Antrim	Deputy Lieutenant Shane O'Neill
Armagh	[Sir Neile O'Neile [[Deputy Lieutenant Con O'Neile
Derry	Colonel Cormuck O'Neile
Tyrone	Colonel Gordon O'Neile

The O'Neill Genealogies

Ui Neill High Kings		Kings of Aileach	
		Inauguration	
Niall	d. 453		
Loeguire	d. 461/3	Niall Glundubh	896
Coirpre	d. ?	Flaithbertach	916
Muircheartach	d. 534/6	Fergal	919
Forggus	d. 566	Muircheartach	938
Domnall		Domnall	943
Baetan		Flaithbertach	943
Eochaid		(son of Muircheartach)	
Colman Rimid	c. 604	Flaithbertach	953
Suibne Menn	d. 628	(son of Conchobair)	
Fergal	d. 722	Aed	989
Aed Allan	d. 743	Flaithbertach	1004
Niall Frossach	d. 778	Aed	1030
Aed Oirdnide	d. 819	Domnall	1067
Niall Caille	d. 846	Aed	1068
Aed Findliath	d. 879	Donnchad	1083
Niall Glundubh	d. 919	Aed	1167

* N.B. The name Aed = Aedh = Aodh = Hugh

O'Neills. Kings of Tir Eoghain

Earls of Tyrone and "The O'Neills"

Inauguration

Brian	1238
Niall Culanach	1261
Domnall	1283
Brian	1291
Enri	1325
Aodh	1345
Niall Mor	1364
Niall Og	1397
Brian Og	1403
Domhnall	1404
Eoghan	1410
Enri	1455 + Aodh
Conn	1483
Enri Og	1493 "The O'Neills of the Fews", Armagh, Mayo and
Domhnall	1498 Leitrim
Art	1509
Art Og	1513 * To Don Carlos O'Neill, "The O Neill Mor"
* Conn Bacach	1519 of Sevilla, Spain, 1990
* Sean an Diomuis	1559

Toirdhealbhach
(Turlough Luineach) 1567   Conn
* Aodh (The Great) 1593   Art Og
    | Sean   b. 1599
* To Conde de Tiron (Spain)   Thomas   b. 1619
                                    Tadgh/
                                    Teige   b. 1641
                                    Henry O'Neill/Payne/
                                        Paine
                                        |
                        * To Robert O'Neill/Paine
                            Farranavane, Cork
                                   c. 1887
                                \|/

O'Neills of Clann Aodha Buidhe

Starts at Brian	1347
Domhnall Og died	1234
Aodh Buidhe	

|

Inauguration Date

Brian	1347
Muircheartach	1395
Brian Ballach	1395
Aodh Buidhe	1425
Muircheartach	1444
Conn	1468
Niall Mor	1482
Aodh Buidhe	1512
Brian Ballach	1542
Fedhlimidh Bacach	1529
Niall Og	1533
Muircheartach	1537

|

| |

O'Neills of Upper (Clanaboy)   O'Neills of (Lower Clanaboy)

O'Neills of Upper (Clanaboy)		O'Neills of (Lower Clanaboy)	
Aodh	c.1533	Muircheartach	c.1533
Fedhlimidh Dubh	1556	Sir Brian	1556
Sir Conn	1556	Aodh	1574
Niall	1590	Aodh Og	1583
Eoghan	1601	Sir Sean	c.1595

* <u>To</u> Hugo O'Neill, "O'Neill of Clann
Aodha Buidhe", 1990

The O'Neill of Clannabuidhe Inauguration Chair; now in the Ulster Museum.

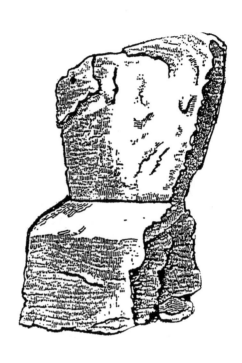

The last O'Neill inaugurated on this chair during the reign of English King, James I, was Con O'Neill. A Brian Phelim O'Neill had his land taken from him in 1574 and it was divided up between his two sons, Shane and Con. These Clanaboy O'Neills became Protestants and gradually began to lose contact with their Gaelic-Irish heritage. They did well until 1798 when Viscount O'Neill was killed by " insurgents ". After that, a serious lack of prodigy in this O'Neill family led to distant relations of a Mary O'Neill, the Chichesters, inheriting the O'Neill lands in 1868. These Chichesters changed their name by Royal Licence to O'Neill and took the arms of O'Neill. The first inheritor, the Reverend William Chichester was created Baron O'Neill in 1868. He was a Prebendary of St. Michael's in Dublin. His descendants have included Terence O'Neill, Lord O'Neill of the Maine, former Prime Minister of Northern Ireland and the Barons O'Neill of Shane's Castle. These O'Neills are friendly with the O'Neills in Portugal and were responsible for organising the inauguration of the late " O'Neill of Clannabuidhe ", the inauguration of whose son Hugo O'Neill is due to take place at Shane's Castle in the summer of 1991.

The Main Genealogy of the O'Neill of Magh Da Chonn (as of 1991)

Cu Chorb, King of Leinster,

Nia Corb, eldest son.

Cormac Gealta Gaoth.

Feidhlimidh Firurghlais.

Cathair Mor, High King, c.177   Fedlimthe Rechtmair, High King c.164

Fiachu ba hAiccid   Fiacha Suighde

Bressal Belach, King of Leinster   Artchorp

Labrado Laidig, died 446   Oengus, "of the dread lance"

Enda Cennselach a Quo Ui Chennselaig

                                                        Ercbran, King of the Deise

Crimthann, King of Leinster = Mell (daughter of Ercbran)

Nath I, King of Leinster for 10 years, died 494

Ailill

Fhergusa

Bresail

Fhergaile

Neill A Quo O'Neills of Magh Da Chonn

Cinaeda

Cernach (Lord of Ui Bairrche, died c.856)

O'Neill of Magh Da Chonn, Caithreim Ceallachan Caisil, c.934-44
(Domnall ua O'Neill)

O'Neill of Magh Da Chonn, Annals of the Four Masters, c. 1087

O'Neill of Magh Da Chonn, Topographical Poem, c. 1400

Prior O'Neill , of Kilcarry. c. 1500 - 1552

Art Mac Prior c. 1552 - Eoghan Mac Art c. 1552
Niall Mac Prior c. 1552 - Donaill, Aodh and Donagh
                             Mac Niall c. 1571-1625
Donaill Mac Prior c. 1552 - Aodh and Brian Mac Donaill
                               c. 1575-1583

Niall Mac Prior O'Neill, had to sign over wood in Clonegal to the Earl of Kildare, c. 1572
Donagh Mac Niall O'Neill, had to give rights to Morgan Mac Brian Kavanagh, on land in what is now St. Mullins Upper, Co. Carlow, but which was Fearann ui Neill, c. 1604

(There are also six other family trees from this period)

Genealogy of Don Carlos O'Neill, "O Neill Mor"

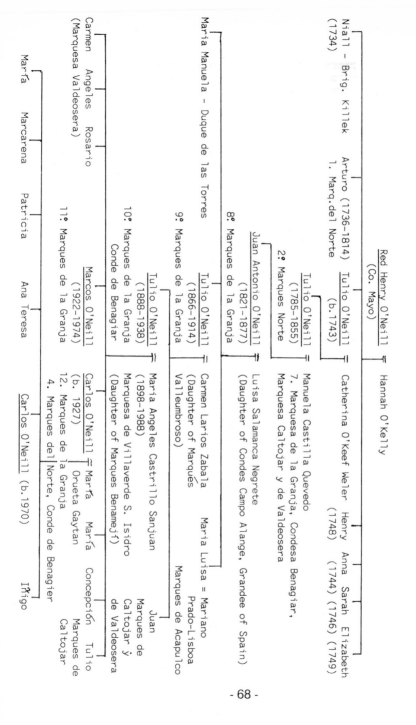

Red Henry O'Neill
(Co. Mayo)
=
Hannah O'Kelly

Niall – Brig. Killek (1734)

Arturo (1736–1814)
1. Marq. del Norte
=
Catherina O'Keef Weler (1748)

Henry (1744)   Anna (1746)   Sarah (1749)   Elizabeth

Tulio O'Neill (b.1743)
2º Marques Norte
=
Manuela Castilla Quevedo
7. Marquesa de la Granja, Condesa Benagiar,
Marquesa Caltojar y de Valdeosera

Tulio O'Neill (1785–1855)

Juan Antonio O'Neill (1821–1877)
8º Marques de la Granja
=
Luisa Salamanca Negrete
(Daughter of Condes Campo Alange, Grandee of Spain)

Maria Manuela – Duque de las Torres

Tulio O'Neill (1866–1914)
9º Marques de la Granja
=
Carmen Larios Zabala
(Daughter of Marques Valleumbroso)

Maria Luisa = Mariano
Prado–Lisboa
Marques de Acapulco

Tulio O'Neill (1888–1938)
10º Marques de la Granja
Conde de Benagiar
=
Maria Angeles Castrillo Sanjuan (1898–1988)
Marquesa de Villaverde S. Isidro
(Daughter of Marques Benagí)

Juan
Marques de
Caltojar y
de Valdeosera

Carmen Angeles Rosario
(Marquesa Valdeosera)

Marcos O'Neill (1922–1974)
11º Marques de la Granja
=
Carlos O'Neill (b. 1927)
12. Marques de la Granja
4. Marques del Norte, Conde de Benagier

María
Orueta Gaytan

María Concepción
Marques de
Caltojar

Tulio

Carmen   Marcarena   Patricia   Ana Teresa

Carlos O'Neill (b.1970)   Iñigo

Chief O'Neill's Favourite

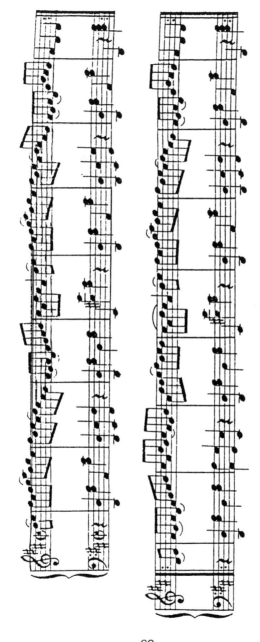

One of 400 tunes in Capt. Francis O'Neill's. "O'Neill's Irish Music", arranged by Selena O'Neill, B. Mus.. (Published by kind permission of Mercier Press, Dublin and Cork)

Some Books relating to the O'Neills

Burke, Sir Bernard. Burke's Peerage and Burke's Landed Gentry of Ireland, London 1912-1970.

Burke, Sir Bernard. Shane's Castle.

Casway, Jerrod. Owen O'Neill and the Struggle for Catholic Ireland.

Curley, Walter P. Monarchs in Waiting, New York, 1973.

Holohan, Renagh. The Irish Chateaux, Dublin 1989.

Mathews, Anthony. Origin of the O'Neills, Ulster, 1971.

Mathews, Thomas. The O'Neills of Ulster: Their History & Genealogy, in 3 vols. Dublin, 1907.

Mitchell, John. The Life and Times of Hugh O'Neill, 1868.

O'Cahan, T.S. Owen Roe O'Neill

O'Donovan, John. The Annals of the Four Masters

O'Faolain, Sean. The Great O'Neill

O'Hart, John. Irish Pedigrees, New York, 1923

O'Neill, Eoghan. Gleann an Oir (O'Neills of Uibh Eoghain Fhinn)

O'Neill, Sean. The O'Neills of Leinster, 1991

O'Neill, Viscount. Genealogical History of the Ancient House of O'Neill, MSS 16006, National Library, Dublin.

Peander, Seamus. Census of Ireland.

Walsh, Rev. Paul. The Will and Family of Hugh O'Neill, Earl of Tyrone, Dublin 1930.

Walsh, Rev. Paul. Irish Chiefs & Leaders, Dublin 1960.

Walsh, Micheline Kerney. The O'Neills of Spain, Destruction by Peace & Spanish Knights of Irish Origin (O'Donnell Lectures), Dublin 1960.

Williams, J.D. The Name of O'Neill, Cork, 1978.

Woulfe, Patrick. Sloinnte Gaedhael is Gall.

Some Journals Containing O'Neill Material

Duiche Neill, O'Neill Country Historical Societies Journal, Nos. 1-5, 1989-91

Ulster Journal of Archeology, The Making of an O'Neill by Hayes-McCoy, Vol.33, 1970

Weekly Irish Times, The Tyrone Baganal Affair by J.C. Weir, K.C., LL.D., Mar 12, 1904

Irish Family Links, Belfast - Ongoing.